UNDER

AN   GS

"See that you despise not one of these little ones: for I say to you, that their angels in heaven always see the face of my Father who is in heaven."

—Matthew 18:10

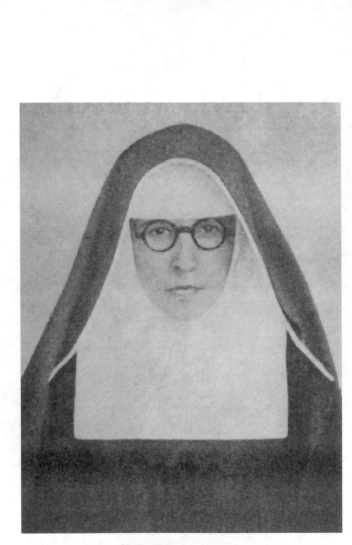

Sister Maria Antonia
(Cecy Cony)
1900-1939

UNDER ANGEL WINGS

THE TRUE STORY OF A YOUNG GIRL AND HER GUARDIAN ANGEL

THE AUTOBIOGRAPHY OF
SISTER MARIA ANTONIA
RELIGIOUS OF THE SISTERS OF ST. FRANCIS
OF PENANCE AND CHRISTIAN CHARITY

From the original Portuguese edited by
Fr. J. Batista Reus, S.J.

Translated by
Fr. Conall O'Leary, O.F.M

"For he hath given his angels charge over thee; to keep thee in all thy ways. In their hands they shall bear thee up: lest thou dash thy foot against a stone."
—Psalm 90:11-12

TAN BOOKS AND PUBLISHERS, INC.
Rockford, Illinois 61105

For the English edition:

Imprimi Potest: Celsus Wheeler, O.F.M.
                        Minister Provincial

Nihil Obstat: Bede Babo, O.S.B.
                        Censor

Imprimatur: John J. Dauenhauer
                        Administrator of the Diocese of
                        Paterson, New Jersey
                        April 21, 1953

Retypeset and republished in 2000 by TAN Books and Publishers, Inc. Footnotes are from the original 1953 edition unless marked thus: "—*Publisher*, 2000."

Library of Congress Control No.: 99-70761

ISBN 0-89555-647-2

Printed and bound in the United States of America.

TAN BOOKS AND PUBLISHERS, INC.
P.O. Box 424
Rockford, Illinois 61105

2000

THIS is the story of a privileged Brazilian girl, born in 1900, who was led to high sanctity under the continual guidance, protection and inspiration of her Guardian Angel, whom she called her "New Friend." However, in accordance with the decrees of Urban VIII, the account of the supernatural gifts and revelations of Sister Maria Antonia (Cecy Cony) is to be accepted only on human faith, and everything in this book is submitted to the infallible judgment of the holy Catholic Church.

PUBLISHER'S POSTSCRIPT, 2000

In October of 1999, in response to our inquiry regarding a possible decision by the Church regarding the life and experiences of Sister Maria Antonia, we received a communication from the Provincial Minister of the Franciscan Sisters of Penance and Christian Charity in Porto Allegre/RS, Brazil. The Sister wrote:

"First of all we want to say that it came as a surprise, and a great joy too, to know about your interest in regard to our Sister Antonia Cony, about the research already made of her life and the precise datas gathered.

"As for your question concerning a possible decision made by the Church about the matters in question, nothing has happened up to now. At the moment it is at a standstill. Nevertheless there are some occasional petitions made by the people asking for more publication and more disclosure of datas of Sister Maria Antonia's life.

"We are keeping the number of your fax and, if anything comes up, we will be happy to inform you . . ."

Contents

Contents

Translator's Preface

One day in Rio de Janeiro when I was looking through the books in the shop conducted by Vozes, the Franciscan publishing house, I came upon a book entitled *Devo Narrar Minha Vida,* with the picture of a young Sister on the cover. I included it among the books I was buying, because biographies and autobiographies have always had a special appeal for me. Not long afterward a letter reached me from Mother M. Clarissa, Assistant General of the Sisters of St. Francis of Penance and Christian Charity. Mother Clarissa was seeking an English translator for this autobiography. Mother mentioned in her letter that translations were being prepared in Dutch and German, and that a Dutch Franciscan had been instrumental in introducing Sister Maria Antonia's cause in Rome. After examining the book I was glad to accept the task of translating it into English. Now that this work is finished, I consider it a great privilege to bring to English readers knowledge of this favored soul, so innocent, so childlike, so marvelously protected by her Guardian Angel, whom she calls her New Friend.

Sister Maria Antonia was the daughter of João Ludgero de Aguiar Cony, a captain in the Brazilian army, and his wife, Antonia Soares Cony. Born in 1900, she was baptized Cecy, a name which is probably a derivative of Cecilia.* In the intimate circle of her family and friends, she was known by the nickname Dédé.

The autobiography of Sister Maria Antonia was first published in 1949 by the Franciscan Press of Petropolis, Brazil. This book became so popular that the first edition was soon exhausted, and a second edition was issued in 1950. The editor of the autobiography was Father John Baptist Reus, S.J., who had been Sister Maria Antonia's spiritual director during the closing years of her life. In his introduction Father Reus tells us how the autobiography came to be written:

> Obliged by obedience, Sister Maria Antonia wrote the recollections of her life, with a certain repugnance and after asking the special help of Our Lord. According as she finished each of the six notebooks of which the autobiography consists, she handed them in to her superiors, and did not ask anything further about them. She died before she could finish her autobiography, which describes her life only up to her twenty-first year.

---

*Thus, in English the name *Cecy* would presumably be pronounced *See-see*. —*Publisher*, 2000.

Sister Maria Antonia was able to appear before Our Lord in all the radiant beauty of her baptismal innocence.

The manuscript was read by several persons, who found it so appealing that they asked to have it published so that others might draw inspiration from it. The facts narrated in this autobiography deserve the belief of any prudent person who is versed in these matters. Sister Maria Antonia was intelligent and well educated. In her classes, she was usually in first or second place. In the exercise of her profession her superiors testify that she was an excellent teacher.

Humble, singularly sincere and innocent, she never lied in her life. She never offended her Divine Master deliberately [*"por querer"*]. This phrase gives us the key by which we can judge correctly certain external faults noted in her by certain persons. She was incapable of inventing mystical occurrences. Neither from books nor in any other ordinary way could she have become acquainted with the supernatural phenomena that she describes so clearly. When she learned toward the end of her life that there were souls who never experienced the sensible presence of Our Lord at Holy Communion, she asked with surprise:

"Not even on the day of their First Holy Communion?" When she received an answer in the negative, she wept bitterly, exclaiming: "Those souls never came to know Our Lord in this life."

The late Father Francis X. Zartmann, S.J., had a deep admiration for the life of Sister Maria Antonia. His opinion is of great value to us, because for many years he was Provincial of the Southern Brazilian Province of the Society of Jesus. He had been director of Jesuit priests during their year of tertianship. He was an experienced spiritual director and retreat master for priests and religious, a man of calm and sound judgment, a deep student of mystical phenomena.

It was necessary to omit certain passages from the manuscript which referred to the interior life or to persons who could be identified. Knowledge of her life in the convent was drawn from Sisters who enjoyed the friendship and confidence of Sister Maria Antonia.

Father Reus's introduction is written in the careful, restrained language of the professor of theology. Along more lyrical lines, another tribute to Sister Maria Antonia comes from the eloquent pen of His Excellency Dom Frei Henrique Golland Trindade, O.F.M., who wrote the Preface to the Portuguese work. Dom Henrique says:

Along with the familiarity which this holy Franciscan Sister enjoyed with her Guardian Angel, the most profound impression that we received from reading this autobiography was the simplicity, the ingenuousness, of the whole narration. For us this is one of the proofs of its truthfulness. One cannot imitate such a style. It is written in the language of the *Fioretti* of St. Francis. It is like a humble and unpretentious stream flowing through the fields and the woods, murmuring:

"Whoever wishes to seek me,
   Let him do so!
Whoever wishes to approach and
     contemplate me,
   Let him do so!
Whoever wishes to drink from my
     waters,
   Let him do so!
Whoever wishes to believe in me,
   Let him do so!
I am nothing but a stream
     flowing along,
   Touched by the Angels,
Illuminated by the sun in God's
     Heaven."

How wonderful it is to read pages such as these, pages capable of raising the level of our spiritual life, which is so weak, so earthly! We must convince ourselves that Our Lord is still generous with His gifts, that He has not yet closed His sacred hands and heart. He still seeks souls who will listen to Him. He is still the Eternal Beggar, knocking, knocking at the door of our hearts, with His hair wet with dew from the long nights when He has been spurned by His creatures who do not love Him, who do not want Him. Yet He continues to knock and to wait.

Not only in the convents but in every place where human beings dwell, He knocks: in homes, factories, colleges, business houses. In every place there can exist souls living a true mystical life, living in intimate union with Our Lord. To cite examples: mothers and wives like Anna Maria Taigi and Elizabeth Leseur; workers like Matt Talbot; university professors like Contardo Ferrini; business people like Marie Guyard before her entrance into the Ursulines; seamstresses like Marie Eustelle . . .

In the ranks of these and of many others, Sister Maria Antonia now takes her place. Teacher, Franciscan Sister, native

of the state of Rio Grande do Sul, she
lived in our own day. Let us rejoice! Let
us also be convinced that the mystical
life, with all its graces, surrounds us in
every place. Only let our souls be pure,
humble, recollected! Let us open the
door of our souls to the knocking of
divine love, and our Divine Master and
Spouse will enter and will sup with us!
Then the Father, the Word and the Holy
Spirit will make our souls their dwelling
place.

The world, weighed down and satu-
rated with crimes and sins, lies sunken
in a tremendous abyss. Only mystical
souls, souls of the Cross, souls of divine
love, can balance the scales of divine justice. The world, proud and opinionated,
binds itself in a maze of complications.
Only the simplicity of the Gospel, the
way of spiritual childhood which St.
Thérèse of Lisieux taught and Sister
Maria Antonia lived—only this can save
the world. Visible and invisible devils fill
the cities and the country, homes and
schools, workshops and mansions. Only
the Angels of God, so ignored and forgotten, can triumph over them.

This, then, seems to be the threefold
mission of Sister Maria Antonia: first, to
encourage us to enter the mystical way

of prayer and self-immolation without fear, for only there will we come to know and enjoy God; secondly, to teach us the simplicity of faith; thirdly, to stir up in our hearts a great love for our invisible friends our Guardian Angels.

We offer this autobiography to English readers with the weighty recommendations of these two eminent priests and scholars: John Baptist Reus, S.J., who died in 1947, a one-time professor of theology at the Seminário Central (a regional seminary) in São Leopoldo, state of Rio Grande do Sul; and His Excellency Dom Frei Henrique Golland Trindade, O.F.M., Bishop of Botucatú, famous preacher and author of several books for spiritual reading. We believe that readers will find this autobiography interesting, timely, enlightening, edifying and even humorous. When they have finished, let them thank God for this innocent soul who grew up in our own age, subject to all the evil influences of this century, who was yet guided through it all, safe and unharmed, even as was the younger Tobias, by the Angel of the Lord! Let them also turn their eyes upon the many benefits they have received from day to day from their own Guardian Angels; and let them thank sincerely these invisible, protecting and inspiring friends of ours!

FR. CONALL O'LEARY, O.F.M.

UNDER
ANGEL WINGS

"Behold I will send my angel, who shall go before thee, and keep thee in thy journey, and bring thee into the place that I have prepared . . ."

—Exodus 23:20-22

Sister Maria Antonia did not identify by name some of the companions and friends who enter into her life story. Names have been supplied in these cases by the translator of the autobiography in English. These designations include: Lucy, in Chapter V; Laila, Chapter V; Inácia, Chapter VI; Zita, Chapter VIII; Dona Nayá, Chapter XI; Alice, Chapters XVI and XIX; Elena, Chapter XIX; Sarah, Chapter XXII. With the exception of the aforementioned, all other names are those supplied by the author of the original manuscript.

Chapter 1

My Father in Heaven*

MY GOOD JESUS, I want to fulfill Thy most holy Will. May I, the least of all Thy creatures, glorify Thy name! Remembering everything that Thou hast done for me, O my God, may I love Thee still more! I must narrate everything that I recall about my life. I shall write it as it comes from my heart.

I consider my life as two chains intertwined: one being Divine Grace, and the other the misery of a creature. I was born on the fourth of April in the year 1900, and I remember the years of my childhood from the age of four. I remember so well the town where I was born, Santa Vitória do Palmar, with its extensive groves of palm trees. I remember also my home and the children with whom I played. My memory goes back even to the afternoon of February 2, 1904, when, as I was sitting on the steps that led out to the yard and playing with a little toy

---

*Sister Maria Antonia's manuscript was divided into sections and given headings by the editor of the original Portuguese, Fr. John Baptist Reus, S.J. The division into chapters in the English version is that of the translator.

bear, I heard my father calling to me: "Dédé, come and see the baby which we found in the basket that the big stork carried in his beak to Mother." This was my brother Jandir.

I recall also that even at that time I already had some idea of the good God. I remember the crucifix on the pedestal that was always on top of the high bureau. To see this I had to be lifted up by Acácia, the good nursemaid who took care of me until I was ten or eleven years old. Likewise I remember the big picture representing the Most Holy Trinity, just as I recall the holy water font in honor of the Immaculate Conception. This is all.

I knew the good God by the name "Father of Heaven," and I remember that it was my own father who spoke to me of my heavenly Father.

My Heavenly Father Is Happy

One day there was a great storm, and my father was sitting in his comfortable armchair, reading something. The thunder and the lightning succeeded each other. Frightened, I ran to the protecting arms of my father, hiding myself between his knees. It was there that my father said to me:

"Are you listening? That is our Father in Heaven, who is angry with those children and grownups who do not want to be good. But when little children are good, our Heavenly

Father is very happy and He commands the sun to shine."

Thus it was that I arrived at an idea of the good God. And from that day until I was six years old, every day as soon as I woke up my first interest was to see whether the sun was shining or whether it was raining. If it was raining, but without thunder, then I imagined that my heavenly Father was sad because of me, but without being angry. And nearly always, if not always, I discovered in myself the reason why my Heavenly Father was sad. Perhaps I had not allowed Acácia to put ringlets in my hair, or I had called her ugly. Or I had cried in anger because I wanted to see the soldier* bathe Congo, the big horse that my father rode. Or I had pretended to eat and had thrown the food on the ground. On that day when in my anger I threw the food on the ground, it rained and thundered.

But always after these tantrums I felt a great disgust with myself for having offended the good God. Then I would run to my mother's bedroom and, looking at the big picture representing the Eternal Father with a long white beard, I would gaze intently at His holy face to see whether He was still sad or angry with me. But never, never, during the three years when

---

*Cecy's father was a captain in the Brazilian army. The soldier was in the service of the Cony family.

this was my custom did I find that the holy face of my Heavenly Father appeared still angry.

Thus it was that I began to love the good God and to desire to please Him, as I thought to myself: "My Heavenly Father is so good, and He wants to do good things for me. When I am bad, He does not like it; but when I tell Him that I will not do such a bad thing any more, then my Heavenly Father is my friend once more."

I never spoke to anyone about this daily custom of mine. Only a few times did I hear anyone speaking about God. I did not know how to pray until I was five years old. This I learned at school. However, I knew that the good God lived in Heaven and that everything which was beautiful and good had been made by Him.

The Crucified and His Holy Mother

Up to this time I had known only about the Father of Heaven with the long beard that was as white as cotton. I had heard no one speak about the meaning of the crucifix on the bureau. In my ignorance I did not like to look at it, because I felt a kind of horror and sorrow for that "unknown Man."

At that time [1904] there resided in Santa Vitória the Reis family. Dona Glória Reis, the last living member of that family today, had opened a private school there. My older sisters were enrolled in this school, and this was the beginning of a close friendship between my parents and the Reis family. One day Dona Mimosa Reis, the mother of Dona Glória, came to our house. My little brother, Jandir, who was only a few months old, was sick; and so Dona Mimosa was taken to my mother's bedroom. I liked this lady very much. As soon as I knew that she was present in the house I would run to her and stay with her as long as she remained. Thus it happened on that day. Hearing the voice of Dona Mimosa, I ran to be with her. Leaning against her knees, I remained with her.

Dona Mimosa was sitting in front of the big bureau, where one could see, in the center, the black crucifix with the white corpus of Christ. Standing up and holding me in her arms, she went to the bureau. Taking down the crucifix, she asked me: "Dédé, do you know who this is?" I did not know what to answer. Then, taking the holy water font representing Our Lady of the Immaculate Conception, she asked the same question, and again I did not know the answer. But when she pointed to the picture of the Most Holy Trinity—ah, then I knew: yes, it was the great Father of Heaven, whom I already loved so much. I remember perfectly, as if it were today, that first simple lesson which I received at the age of four from that good and pious lady, whose image has always remained in my memory. May the good God give her a just reward for the immense good she did for my soul!

When I said to her that the Eternal Father was the Father of Heaven, Dona Mimosa pointed to the crucifix and said:

"*He* also lives in Heaven. He is the Son of the good Father of Heaven. Your name is Cecy, and His name is Jesus. Jesus lives in Heaven, a very beautiful place, which He made. And here on earth, where you live, the Father of Heaven made everything for those who live here. And the Father of Heaven said: 'Those who are good I will take to my beautiful Heaven to live with Me.' But most of the people did not want to be good; and so instead of going to the beautiful Heaven, they would have been sent for punishment to the depths of the earth, which is filled with fire, and which is where the wicked devil lives.

"But the Father of Heaven, being so good, had pity on these bad people. So He sent His Son Jesus to live here on earth, that He might ask all the people to be good and to do only what His Father in Heaven wanted them to do. But many people did not like the good Jesus. They beat Him; they mocked Him; and they sent the soldiers to seize Him. Then they made a cross like this one, but much bigger. And using a great hammer and long nails, they fastened the good Jesus to that great big cross. Jesus died. Afterward, He came to life again and went back to Heaven.

"But Jesus is so good, and He loved those bad people so much that He said to them: 'Do not do bad things! Everyone, even children like Cecy who want to be good, I shall bring to the beautiful Heaven, which is filled with angels who fly like the butterflies.'"

Then, taking the holy water font, Dona Mimosa continued the lesson, saying: "This beautiful woman is the Mother of the good Jesus. She is good like her Son, and went with Him to Heaven." This was the end of the lesson, a most important lesson, which sank into my childish soul and served as my guide for three years.

My Soul's First Great Sorrow

When Dona Mimosa, still holding me, wished to return to the place where she had been sitting, I threw my arms around her neck and began to cry convulsively. My mother and Dona Mimosa were frightened, not knowing the cause of my tears. Then Acácia came and led me away to see Congo, the big horse that I liked so much.

This was the first great sorrow of my soul during my childhood. I felt a great pity for the good Father of Heaven, whom I loved much more from that day forward and whom I always desired to please, even though I might commit thousands and thousands of faults, because not one of those faults was voluntary, especially from the day I received that holy lesson.

The "poor Jesus," nailed on that black cross, had from that time forward a great attraction for and influence over me. I loved God much more now; and many times during the day, but especially when it began to get dark, I would post myself at the foot of that bureau so that Jesus would not be alone and would not be afraid of the soldiers who treated Him so cruelly.

Often Acácia took me away, surprised at my attraction for that bureau, not knowing the true cause for this. That bureau attracted me in spite of the great dread that filled me when the room became dark and silent (since at that hour all were usually out on the veranda). On one occasion, as I shall explain, I was unjustly accused because of being at my favorite post.

The Attraction of the Bureau

In 1905 my father journeyed to Rio de Janeiro. On his return he brought back big boxes of candied fruits. How I loved to eat these as I sat on the little seat of the swing. There I would receive from my father a big banana covered with sugar or perhaps a big piece of orange. When one piece delighted me more than the others, or when I came upon a new fruit, I thought in my innocence that it was the Mother of Heaven who had made these and sent them down to the little children on earth by means of the beautiful Angels, who could fly like butterflies. (In the home of Captain Bezerra* I had already seen a picture which showed a Guardian Angel crossing a bridge with two little children.)

My mother kept these boxes of fruit on top of that big bureau. Before my father had returned with these boxes, I had been accustomed to drag over to the bureau the high chair which I used at table and which was usually in the room next to Mother's bedroom. I could then climb on it and get a close view of the hands and feet of Jesus, with those big nails that caused Him so much pain. Now one evening as it began to grow dark, I started to climb on the chair, as was my custom, without ever thinking of the boxes of fruit. Just then Acácia entered the room and, seeing me, became very angry. Taking me with one hand and the chair in the other, she brought me to my father, at the same time saying to me: "Little glutton, you would take some of that fruit, and then either I or Conceiçao [the other servant] would get the blame! I will tell all about this."

My father looked at me sorrowfully and said: "Now I know that my little girl is like the little

---

*Apparently a friend of the family.

mice, who love to take away what they can find."
I could not say a word. Up to now I had not
known what a lie or an injustice was, and my
limited intelligence could not conceive how
Acácia could accuse me of something that I
had not done. Of course, she had been deceived
by appearances. Shortly afterward, however, I
forgot about this incident, and I continued
faithfully to keep watch before the Crucified,
whom I never forgot, even in the midst of my
playing.

How many times I hid behind the door and
wept profoundly out of pity for Jesus nailed to
that big cross on which He died! My parents
were accustomed to make social visits in the
summertime, and nearly always we children
accompanied them. However, I never felt happy
visiting others, although generally I had other
children to play with. Always in my mind was
the thought that Jesus was alone and that He
would certainly be afraid of those evil soldiers.

The Angel

In the year 1905 the time for the carnival
approached. At that season my mother would
deck us out in fancy dress. Then, accompanied
by Acácia and Conceição, my sisters and I would
go with the other little ones to the town square.
I had a great dread of those who disguised
themselves in those horrible masks. I thought

the masks were their real faces, and I believed that those persons were supernatural beings who lived in the depths of the earth, surrounded by fire, in that place about which Dona Mimosa had spoken.

I believe that this was the first year that I accompanied my sisters. All the confusion and noise of the square frightened me. The multitude of masked people, big and small, jumping around and beating the ground with those big balloons tied at the end of a stick—all this filled me with such terror that I might have died if the good God had not come to my aid. I was with the other children, who were enjoying themselves; but Acácia and Conceição, conversing with other servants, were not paying any attention to me.

Thus, filled with terror and with no one to comfort me, I conceived the idea of getting away from there and returning home. I did not know the way, but I resolved to leave by the big gate. This was all I knew. I did not think of anything else. I left the group of children, and immediately I was swallowed up in that small square, which to me was like a world without end. I did not cry. My great fear had frozen my tears.

In my terror I remembered the good Jesus, whom I had left behind alone, and I felt a great sorrow for not having brought Him with me. But I knew that my Father in Heaven sees and knows everything, and that He certainly saw me there alone. Just then a big man, wearing a horrible mask and with flashing eyes that I can still see in my imagination, approached me and took me by the hand. At that moment I could have died of fright.

I had walked a few steps, held prisoner in his big hand, when I sensed, at my side, without actually seeing anything—knew to be present just as truly as I knew the presence of the big masked man on my other side—the Angel whom I had seen in the picture at the home of Captain Bezerra. My Father in Heaven had sent this angel to stay with me and take me home. I was aware of his presence without seeing him, but it was as if I had seen him. I had the absolute certainty that he was at my side, on the side opposite the masked man. Then the masked man freed me with a push and I did not see him anymore. He disappeared into the crowd.

All my terror now left me, and my soul was filled with a sweet tranquillity because of the confidence I felt in my "New Friend." I had come in sight of the gate leading out of the square when I saw Acácia running toward me. If I had seen her before the arrival of my "New Friend," I should certainly have run toward her with the same anxiety with which she was hastening toward me. But my calmness no doubt quieted Acácia's anxiety; and neither she, nor my father, nor my mother, ever knew of this incident of the Angel, for this is the first time that I have related it.

From that day in February or March of 1905 my "New Friend" accompanied me always and everywhere. He stood guard with me at the foot of the big bureau as we watched before the Crucified Jesus. From that time I had no more fear of the semi-darkness of that room, for I felt the sweet, protecting presence of my "New Friend." That is the name I gave him and called him by until I was six years old, when I learned that he was my holy Guardian Angel. I understood him perfectly when he spoke to me, although I never heard his holy voice.

* * *

O FAITHFUL Guardian of my childhood and girlhood, how great is my longing to see you, my New Friend! Permit me to weep; it will not do any harm. These tears I offer you, my faithful Guardian, as a proof of my great love and my great desire to see you. After thirty years, why have you hidden yourself from your little sister and friend? But you are still with me, I know, even though I have not been aware of your holy company and presence since last year, 1935. As I recall all that you have done for me, I desire to love you still more. If it were not for you, my holy Guide, who knows but that I might have offended my good God voluntarily and gravely, thousands of times! How many, many times, given up to my own caprices and inclinations, I was ready to do evil, when your holy warning arrived, always on time, to hinder me from falling!

The Secret of the Little Basket

Soon after the carnival I heard my father saying one day that we were going to take our vacation at the sea. On the following day I saw Acácia, Conceição and my mother busily preparing clothes and packages. We were going to the sea! This thought delighted me. My New Friend would go also. This I knew. Every member of the household was going, even the good Abelino, the soldier who bathed Congo. Abelino would drive the carriage. However, my father could not go. During our absence he would have to live in the barracks, as our house would be closed up. I was thinking about all this while I was arranging, in a little basket that Dona Mimosa had given me, the teddy bear and also the big doll, which could get into the basket only by sitting down.

Suddenly my great joy was changed into bitter sorrow as I remembered Someone. Even the little teddy bear would go; only my beloved Crucified Jesus would remain alone. He who had sent my New Friend to protect me from the masked man, He would have to remain in the dark, closed-up room. I would willingly have remained with Him, but I knew very well that my mother would not allow this. Ah, but—then the thought came to me—supposing, in place of the doll and the teddy bear, I should take along the crucifix. Acácia had given me the little basket for the doll and the teddy bear, but instead I would take the crucifix without my mother or Acácia knowing anything about it.

I went to the bedroom. Having placed the high chair near the bureau, I was able to reach my Great Friend and place Him in my lap. Then, going to the wardrobe, I took out a small cape and wrapped up that crucifix which I liked so much. It was thus that the crucifix went also to the sea. During the journey I kept the basket with me all the time. When we arrived at the sea, I guarded it at the foot of my little bed. We stayed many days at the seaside, but the crucifix remained always in the little basket. I brought it back to the city and placed it on top of the bureau without my mother or Acácia knowing.

Chapter 2

First Confession
and First Communion

TOWARD the end of 1905 or the middle of 1906, my father was transferred to the garrison of Jaguarão. I believe it was here that the second phase of my life began. Soon after our arrival we were enrolled in the School of the Immaculate Conception. I remember my first day at school. Conceição brought us there. Sister Eugene welcomed us, and she was so good and kind that I soon learned to be very fond of her. She took us to her classroom and seated my two sisters and me on the first bench. Then she asked us many things. I was admiring her all the while, as I had never before seen a Sister, and I believe that there was nothing about her person that I did not notice.

What held my attention most was the cross of black cloth which was sewed to her habit, but which did not include the figure of the Crucified. Ah, but in the classroom, hanging from the wall, was a big figure of the Crucified nailed to a cross as big as I was. His hands and feet were stained with blood, and in His side was a great open wound. Poor Jesus! A great sorrow filled my soul and I began to cry. Sister Eugene tried to console me, thinking my tears were caused by my being away from my father and mother.

Then the pupils began to arrive, and the seats filled up quickly with children whom I had never seen before. A short while after this, Sister Eugene led me away to another classroom, while my sisters remained where they were. In this second classroom I found another "girl" sitting at the teacher's desk, and she was dressed just like the Sister who accompanied me. She, too, wore the little cross of black cloth on her breast. On the wall, also, was another figure of the Crucified, hanging from a great cross. And also, to my great joy, I saw on the wall a big picture of my New Friend, a picture just like the one in Captain Bezerra's home. My teacher was the beloved Mother Raphael. She seated me on the first bench, which was to be my place. My New Friend was at my side; I did not need to look for him. Timid and fearful by nature, I remained quiet during the whole time. However, I liked the school and the good "girls" or teachers, whom my father told me I should call "Sisters" and not "girls."

In a short time I knew how to make the Sign of the Cross, to recite the *Our Father*, the *Hail Mary*, the *Creed* and a beautiful prayer to my New Friend. It was Sister Paulina who taught us these. It was here that I learned that my New

Friend was my holy Guardian Angel. Mother
Raphael spoke to us frequently about our good
Father in Heaven, although she never used that
name. She caused me great surprise by calling
Him always the "good God." This made me realize that my Father in Heaven was called God.
I learned also that the Mother of Heaven was
called most holy Mary. Mother Raphael spoke
to us afterward about the good Jesus, whose
holy name I had learned from Dona Mimosa.
She spoke also about the soul, about horrible
sin, about Heaven, Hell and Purgatory. I kept
all these things in my mind, in so far as my
limited intelligence would allow. I knew that my
Guardian Angel would take care of the rest.

The Little White Host

What made the greatest impression on me
was when the good Mother spoke to us of the
little white Host, which contains the same good
God, the same Jesus who lived and died here
on our earth. Soon I was thinking: "If I could
have with me the good Jesus hidden in the little Host, ah, then I would quickly exchange the
little black cross with Jesus nailed on it for the
little white Host, which is truly the living Jesus,
whereas the figure of Jesus on the little cross
is only His image."

I know that I loved the little white Host very
much. On Sundays and holydays of obligation,

I was delighted when I accompanied the Sisters and the other children to the church to pray to the little white Host.

After some months had passed, I knew how to read alone. Then one day Sister Irene came to our classroom and said: "All those who have not made their First Communion, please hold up your hands." I was so happy, as I had already heard Mother Raphael speak about First Communion. I thought of how the good Jesus would come into my little heart and remain always with me. So I, too, raised my hand. Mother Raphael grasped my hand. Still holding on to it, she spoke with Sister Irene. Then, looking at me, Mother Raphael said: "Cecy, you are still very small. You must wait until next year. Your father would not allow you to make your First Communion now. However, you can go with Sister Irene and the other children." This meant that Mother Raphael gave me permission only to assist at the instructions for First Communion.

I felt great disappointment in my soul, a great sorrow and pain. I became very sad, and for the first time I felt unhappy. I thought perhaps Sister Irene would allow me, as she appeared more willing and had even said to me, "Now you ask your father and we shall see." But Mother Raphael, whom I considered more as a friend of mine than Sister Irene, did not want to give me the good Jesus. A sorrowful complaint went up from my heart to my New Friend, who was there beside me, very quiet, not saying anything, but hearing everything.

Ah, my dear Mother Raphael, this was the only complaint I ever had against you during the eleven long years of our association. An unjust complaint, it is true; but it was made by a little heart that loved you very much but did not understand your holy intentions. It was made by a little heart that already had a great love for the little white Host, which you yourself had taught me to know and love.

Hatred of Sin

I began to assist at the instructions given by Sister Irene. Day by day the desire grew to receive the good Jesus into my heart. I felt a great terror for sin, which was so disgusting and displeasing to the good God. Each day, on arising, I said to my New Friend: "My New Friend, my holy Guardian Angel, take good care of me today and do not let me displease the good God. Amen." This was a little prayer that I myself had composed. I repeated it every day of my life, beginning with that day when Sister Irene spoke to us about the good Jesus dying because of the sins of all mankind. I could never forget those words which Sister had used: "Each sin that a person commits is a great big thorn which that person hammers into the sacred head of the good Jesus."

And again she had said: "If we commit a big sin after we have received Jesus into our hearts, then we forcibly drive the good Jesus out of our hearts and allow the devil to enter." These words, which engraved themselves deeply on my soul, aroused in me a real horror of sin. Ah, how many times was I just about to hammer "a great big thorn" into the sacred head of our Divine Lord, when invariably my New Friend would warn me of what I was about to do! From this sprang the consoling and secure confidence that I always placed in him.

The Temptation of the Peaches

One afternoon some other children and my sisters and I went for a walk in the country with Acácia and Conceição. Acácia took money with her to buy fruit, and we carried little baskets. We went to a farm that was recommended by Abelino, the good soldier whom my father had brought with him from Santa Vitória. Abelino conducted us to the farm.

When we arrived at the farm, a man with a hoe on his shoulder told us to enter. We ran into the orchard with Abelino, Acácia and Conceição. While the man was gathering the fruit for Acácia, the other children, without the knowledge of our three guides, began to gather big peaches and plums, which they placed in their baskets. I saw them plainly. Their little baskets were nearly full, and only mine was empty. Just then I was standing under a peach tree. Looking up, I saw a big peach, and another, and another—all within reach of my hand. I thought: "Why cannot I pick some peaches like the other children?" I stretched out my hand to pick a peach, and my fingers had already touched this big velvety peach, when I received the most sweet, calm warning of my New Friend. My arm, suspended in mid-air, was gently lowered by an "invisible hand," which I felt as really as if I had been touched by one of the persons I could see. For I had a better and more clear understanding of the voice of my New Friend than of the spoken words of Mother Raphael, or Sister Pauline, or Sister Irene, whom I could see when they spoke to me.

I repented immediately and with great sorrow of the big ugly sin that I was about to commit; and a great pity for the good Jesus filled my heart as I thought of the great big thorn that I had nearly hammered into His sacred head. That night, as I lay in bed, I wept bitterly after I had begged forgiveness from the good Jesus, from Our Lady and from my New Friend. (This custom of begging forgiveness of my New Friend I kept up until I was fourteen years old.)

In one of her instructions Sister Irene had spoken to us about a young boy who died and was sentenced to suffer in Purgatory because of the lies he had told during life. Up to that time I had not known the meaning of a lie, and I imagined that the poor boy had committed a very big sin to deserve such a punishment. However, my New Friend would give me the explanation very soon.

The Broken Glass

Each afternoon I was accustomed to go with Acácia and the neighborhood children to buy milk. Each child brought along a little glass wrapped in a napkin. I had a very pretty green glass decorated with a golden wing and spotted with little stars. It was Captain Barcelos* who had given it to me.

One of my companions took a great liking to my glass and said to me, "Give me your glass and you can drink milk from mine." Acácia, overhearing this, said, "No, my little lady, each one must drink milk from her own glass." My companion made no answer, and it seemed that she accepted the denial without bitterness. We continued walking for a short time when suddenly my companion turned toward me and gave a violent tug to my napkin, so that the glass fell to the ground and broke into little pieces. With the same speed that she did this she ran toward Acácia, who had gone ahead of

---

*Another family friend, presumably.

us, and said: "Acácia, Cecy was in such a rage because you did not allow her to exchange glasses with me that she just threw hers on the ground and broke it purposely." Naturally, Acácia was highly indignant and she said to me: "What a beautiful way to act, my little angry puppy! Now you can do without a glass and without milk. While the others drink milk, you can watch them!"

Everything happened so quickly that it was all over before I realized what had happened. But then I became so angry and revengeful that I was just about to run after my companion in order to break *her* glass, when my New Friend entered into action, holding me back in the same manner as when he hindered me from stealing the fruit. And I heard clearly the warning of my New Friend: "Your poor companion has committed two big sins." The first, which referred to the breaking of the glass, I did not at that time understand. But the second—ah, I suddenly understood that the second sin was the lie told to Acácia, the same kind of sin for which the young boy was punished. Yes, my companion had lied to Acácia, who thought that everything had happened as it was told to her. Now I understood perfectly the meaning of a lie. I said to my New Friend: "Now I know. It would be a lie if I were to break a glass and afterward tell my mother I did not do it."

We finally arrived at the place where we were

accustomed to buy the milk, and I forgot to tell Acácia that it was not I who had broken the glass. Perhaps it was because my New Friend was with me and I respected his presence even more than I respected the presence of Mother Raphael, Sister Irene and Sister Pauline, the authority of these being supreme in my eyes. Acácia, however, always allowed me to have what I wanted; so she gave me milk from my sister's glass.

Thus it was that my New Friend hindered me from committing the ugly and low sin of vengeance.

*   *   *

O MY holy Guardian Angel, if I were to tell all that you have done for me, a big book would not contain the account of all your holy inspirations.

Modesty, the Handmaid of Purity

If my New Friend had not filled me with the greatest respect for his holy presence, I think that I should have acquired at an early age careless habits, more or less immodest. I realized perfectly well, when I was in the presence of the Sisters or of other persons for whom I had great respect, that I should be careful of the postures I assumed. But I learned to be even more careful when I was alone, for then I felt myself being observed by my New Friend.

Until I was eight years of age it was Acácia who dressed and bathed me, combed my hair, put me to bed and called me in the morning. I had learned to rely on her too much; so it was not until I was ten or eleven that I dispensed completely with her services in this regard. Oftentimes, on getting up in the morning and dressing myself—for example, putting on my stockings—I was not careful of my position or of my dress. At such times I immediately felt the holy presence of my Guardian Angel so vividly, without ever seeing him, and I so strongly felt his reproval of my improper posture, that, being thoroughly ashamed, I would close my eyes lest I see his holy face regarding me sternly.

This scene was repeated innumerable times, sometimes when I was alone, other times when I was in the midst of the most interesting games. Through the grace of the good God I do not remember ever resisting these holy warnings of my New Friend, even though oftentimes I had to subdue my rebellious nature, filled with bad inclinations as it was.

On one occasion my father took us to see a military celebration in Rio Grande do Sul. I was delighted when I saw that there anyone could ride on horseback. Women and children were doing it. I had never ridden except once or twice when my father had seated me on his horse, Congo. At this celebration, I had my heart set on riding. A certain lieutenant was taking care of me, and he brought me a beautiful little pony. This filled me with happiness. He placed me astride the pony as if I were a boy, and I had just begun to pull on the reins when I heard and felt the warning of my New Friend just as vividly as I heard and perceived the lieutenant.*

My New Friend did not want me to continue any farther. I felt his holy arm taking me gently from the pony, just as I had previously felt the lieutenant lifting me onto the pony's back. When I reached the ground, I said to the lieutenant: "I do not wish to ride any more." The lieutenant admired my seeming agility in dismounting from the pony, and he related the fact to my father, who called me cowardly and silly. I should have liked to ride on the pony, but I wanted much more to please my New Friend.

A Bouquet of White Roses for Our Lady

The month of October was approaching and I had not yet obtained permission to make my First Holy Communion. Many times Sister Irene told me to wait after class in order to ask the

---

*Since God had chosen Cecy for intimate union with Himself during her earthly life, her Guardian Angel was charged with the duty of preserving her from the danger of even the slightest fault against modesty.

good Mother for the necessary permission, but Mother Raphael's answer was always evasive. The truth was that externally, in my physical appearance, I seemed to be a child of four or five years. I believe, however, that the true cause for permission being withheld was that I was very slow in class; or, truer still, to speak frankly and sincerely, I was no more than a simpleton. Yet, in spite of my lack of intelligence, I knew very well that Jesus was present in the little white Host, and I loved the Holy Eucharist so much. If my beloved Mother Raphael had only known that every night after the light was put out I buried my head in the pillow in order to hide my sobbing, weeping bitterly because I could not receive the holy visit of my Great Friend, the good Jesus, who suffered so much for me that He might one day bring me to His beautiful home in Heaven!

My New Friend was the only one who shared my secret. There he was, always wide awake; I knew that he was never sleepy. At whatever hour of the night I woke up, he was at my side. After weeping, I would sit up in bed and tell him the reason for my tears. I would finish by beseeching him to intercede for me with the good Mother, as she would certainly do whatever he, the holy Angel, asked of her. And so I would grow calm and consoled by the sweet hope that Mother Raphael would give me permission, and then I would fall asleep.

One such night, as I sat in bed weeping, and as I began to make my customary complaint to my New Friend, suddenly the thought came to me: "Ah! I have forgotten to ask the holy Mother of the good Jesus, Our Lady, whom Sister Irene calls the good Mother of Heaven. If I ask the Mother of Heaven, she will command Mother Raphael to let me make my First Holy Communion."

Early the following morning, as soon as I awoke, I jumped out of bed and went to the foot of the bureau, which was no longer in my mother's bedroom but in the room next to mine. I had not yet grown tall enough to reach the top of the bureau, but I was able to see the little font containing Our Lady's image. I can still remember the prayer I said that morning to Our Lady; it went like this. "Beloved and good Lady, I want so much to receive your Son Jesus into my heart. But Mother Raphael will not allow me, because I am too small. Dear Lady, please make me grow enough today, and command Mother Raphael to notice it. In my money bank I have eight cruzeiros that I saved in order to buy the black drink which is sold in the Girls' Shop. I will not buy this drink, but instead I will spend all this money at the flower shop for a bouquet of big white roses to decorate your altar in the church, if Mother Raphael will give me permission. Amen."

My New Friend was there with me, and I knew

very well that he also wanted our Divine Lord to come into my heart. After making my petition to Our Lady, I returned to my own room to await the coming of Acácia. After breakfast I went to school. It seemed to me that on that day Mother Raphael did not notice how I had "grown," because she said nothing. (I myself was convinced that Our Lady had made me grow.)

On the following day Mother Raphael still did not take any notice of my "new growth." Another day passed by, and another, and still another, yet Mother Raphael did not say anything to me. Finally, I resolved to ask Mother once again for permission to make my First Communion. After class I took up my position at a door through which she had to pass. My heart was beating so violently that I thought I would not be able to speak. But I knew that my New Friend was with me and that he would teach me how to ask.

However, I did not even have to speak. Before I could say a word, Mother Raphael said: "Cecy, I already know what you want. Very well, if your father will give permission, I will also give you permission." If it were not for the great respect that I had for my beloved Mother Raphael, I would have embraced her and caressed her in a thousand ways, even as I was accustomed to do with my father and mother and Acácia when they granted my wishes. But all I could say to

Mother Raphael was, "Yes, Mother, thank you very much." I knew that my father would do whatever I wanted. And if my father granted permission, my mother would do the same. And thus it was.

As it was already late in the afternoon, I could not go to the flower shop to buy the roses for Our Lady. Instead I went to the foot of the bureau and I asked Our Lady to wait until the following day. I took the little font into my hands and kissed the image of the Blessed Mother repeatedly, thus trying to show the good Mother of Heaven how grateful I was to her for having made me grow in such a noticeable manner. (I do not know whether I really did grow. I only know that I was convinced that I had grown, and that I believed it was because of this fact that Mother Raphael had granted permission.)

On the following day I fulfilled my promise. Acácia accompanied me to the flower shop. I said only that I wanted to buy some big white roses for our Blessed Mother's altar in the church. I opened my bank, which was in the shape of a Noah's ark, and I put all the money in my purse. How happy I felt on the return trip as I sat in the boat with Acácia and held the beautiful bouquet of white roses while we were crossing the river. The girl in the flower shop had said: "The bouquet would be more beautiful with 'Black Prince' and 'Queen of Persia.' " Acácia was of the same opinion, but I answered, "No, Miss, I want white roses only." I had promised our Blessed Lady beautiful white roses, a bouquet composed only of white roses, and that is what I brought her.

Padre Domingos* was in the parish church when we got there, and he placed in a big vase the bouquet of white roses belonging to the Mother of Heaven. I felt so happy, immensely happy. That night after retiring, I sat up in my little bed, now not to complain to my New Friend about Mother Raphael but to ask him if Our Lady and he himself had liked the bouquet of white roses. My Noah's ark was empty, and I could not now buy that enticing drink, black as coal, which I had set my heart on buying. However, I began once more to save the coins that my father gave me, and I asked my New Friend not to allow any other girl to buy the black drink until I should have enough money to do so.

But when I had saved a fair number of coins in my Noah's ark, I emptied it a second time, not to buy the coveted black drink but to make another purchase which caused me to feel just as happy as when I bought the white roses. This is a story I shall relate later.

---

*The pastor of the parish.

First Confession

The days of preparation were passing by, and I had already learned from Sister Irene that we must prepare ourselves very well and keep our hearts pure and clean for the visit of the good and loving Jesus. I was already anxious to make my first Confession so that my heart and my soul would become whiter than the beautiful white dress which my mother had ordered. Finally the day of our first Confession arrived. I made my Confession to the rector of the *giná-sio*, Padre Luís Lembrecht. The evening before, in her zeal, Sister Irene had taken us to an empty classroom. There she gave us paper and pencils and told us to write down our sins with the aid of the catechism. My New Friend was there with me, but he did not say anything to me. I thought I should like to be alone with my New Friend. One of the girls sitting beside me would not remain quiet. Every minute or so she would point her finger at one of the sins in the catechism, and she would ask me: "Cecy, are you going to write down this sin?" Each time I answered her: "Sister Irene said that you should tell your sins only to the priest, but yes, I will write that down. It will be better that way."

Sister Irene noticed that my companion was not remaining quiet; so she put her in another seat. And I thought: "Very good, I shall be alone in this bench with my New Friend." I thought and thought. I asked my New Friend to help me make a good Confession. After reading the sins against each commandment, I thought to myself: "There are so many sins here that I have committed; there are others that I am not certain of, and still others that I do not know the meaning of. How many thorns were driven into the sacred head of the good Jesus by all these sins!" As I thought of this, I felt a great sorrow for Jesus. And wishing to console Him, I promised Him, as I struggled to keep from weeping: "O Jesus, never, never more will I be bad. I do not want to commit any more sins, yet I am so tempted to commit sin. But my New Friend watches over me and does not allow me to sin."

Then Sister Irene, who was watching everybody, approached me and said, "Cecy, the others are nearly finished and you have not even begun." So I began immediately, resolving to write down all the sins in the catechism, for I reasoned: "Our Lord knows the sins that I have committed and those that I did not commit. By writing them all down, no sin, no stain of sin, will remain in my heart; and my soul will be as white as the little white Host that I am going to receive."

When all were finished, Sister Irene gave each one an envelope. Then, folding each one's list of sins, she placed them in envelopes, which she sealed. After this she wrote each one's name on the proper envelope. Then she herself kept them until the next day, the day of our first Confession. I went home and I could scarcely wait until the following day. Sister Irene had said: "Tomorrow at two o'clock you will make your first Confession." And so it was.

Finally the great moment arrived. I do not know what various sentiments I experienced. I was not the first to enter the confessional box, for Sister Irene was there to line us up. However, my New Friend was there with me, and I knew that he would enter the box with me. Many times I repeated the Act of Contrition, feeling an enormous sorrow for having offended my heavenly Father. When my turn came, I had in my hand the long list of sins that meant so many big thorns wounding the sacred head of Jesus. I entered the confessional with my heart beating wildly. I was so anxious to tell my sins. I began to read them off. But suddenly the priest stopped me and asked me for the paper. I gave it to him and he kept it. Then I finished my Confession without the help of the paper. The priest questioned me about different sins, and I told him whether I had committed them or not. Even without the paper, which had seemed so indispensable to me before, I knew that I had made an excellent Confession, for I felt happiness such as I had never experienced before.

On leaving the confessional I noticed that the priest was smiling. This increased my happiness, as I thought that he also was pleased with my happiness. It was only later that I understood he was smiling at my simplicity.

After arriving home that afternoon I did not go out to play in the street, as was my custom; nor did I even wish to go to the dairy farm to buy milk, an excursion which I usually enjoyed very much. I was afraid to go out lest in some way I should stain my soul, which was now as bright and beautiful as the veil with its wreath of flowers and the white dress that I was to wear on the morrow. I spent the rest of the afternoon seated in the little rocking chair at the foot of the big bureau, while I recited the Act of Contrition over and over again. No one paid attention to me, except my New Friend, who did not want to go to the dairy farm either. When Acácia returned from the latter place, she showed that she had not forgotten me, for she brought me back some milk in the little blue jug with the painted sheep which my mother had bought for me after the episode of the broken glass.

First Communion and the Sensible Presence of Jesus

The great day of my First Holy Communion, October 17, approached very slowly. Before this great event, we made our second Confession. Finally the eve of the holy day arrived. Sister Irene took good care of us. When I returned home, I remained seated in the little rocking chair at the foot of the bureau, preparing the prayers which we should recite in common before and after the visit of Our Lord, as Sister Irene had told us. I did not yet know how to read quickly, and I was accustomed to point out each word with my finger. Sister Irene did not want us to read our prayers, but I wanted to say them perfectly without mispronouncing one word, so that Our Lord could hear and understand me.

This reminds me of the *Key of Heaven*, the beautiful little prayer book with gilded pages which my beloved Mother Raphael gave me and in which she inscribed, in her beautiful handwriting: "Remembrance of your friend, Mother Raphael." This little prayer book I kept for many years, even until I was a young woman. Then I gave it to my sister Adayl, but only after I had carefully cut out the page with the above inscription, which always gave me so much happiness. Mother Raphael was my friend. How this thought filled me with joy! Mother Raphael seemed to divine the joy that filled my young heart because she was my holy friend, for twelve years later, when she was leaving Jaguarão, she gave me a holy card with the same inscription. I was then eighteen years old, and I have kept that holy

card until now. My good and holy Mother, I
have never forgotten how much I owe you. May
the good God reward you for all the spiritual
benefits that came to me through your efforts!

Finally, the seventeenth of October arrived.
For me this was a holy date, a date of infinite
happiness, a date on which I came to know at
first hand—or rather when I welcomed within
myself—the good Jesus, the Lord of Heaven,
whom a few months before I had known only
from the big picture in my mother's bedroom
and from the beloved crucifix on the big bureau.

*   *   *

MY good Jesus, as I look back, what holy longing
fills my soul as I think of how infinitely happy I was
on the day of my First Communion! That was the
first time, O my God, that I felt really and vividly
within myself Thy most holy presence, Thy Real Presence. It was indeed well that I waited for Thee, O
my Jesus, and I was not deceived. I knew that I
would feel Thee in me, not as I perceived and felt
the presence of my New Friend, but as if Thou, O
my God, were I myself, and as if I myself wert Thou.
Thou in me and I in Thee. Thy soul in my soul,
Thy heart in my heart! Two souls in only one soul!
Two hearts in only one heart! The great omnipo-
tent God and His miserable little creature! I do not
know how to describe how much I loved Thee at
that moment, and how much Thou, O great God,
didst love me. Only we two, Jesus and His little
"Dédé," can know this. O good and most faithful

Jesus, thirty long years have passed since then, and still we love each other very much; infinitely more today, is it not so, O my God? From that day I felt always, always, Thy most holy presence in me, until the past year, when Thou didst leave Thy little servant immersed in the most sorrowful abandonment, in the most sorrowful longing. However, may Thy most holy will be fulfilled in Thy little creature! It is true that even in the novitiate Thou didst hide Thyself from me at times, but soon, very soon, I did find Thee.

The Oath of Fidelity

On that sacred day of my First Communion, October 17, 1906, after I had returned home, accompanied not only by my New Friend, but bearing within me my Divine Guest, I desired most ardently to lock myself in my little room and there to remain alone with my God. I had so many things to say to Him, so many favors to ask from Him. I desired to clasp Him to my heart, to protest my love to Him, to make Him innumerable promises. But alas! Acácia was there waiting for me, ready to take me to the house of my grandmother and my godmother. I went with her, but very soon returned home. When Acácia had taken off my white dress and the veil with its wreath of flowers, I asked her to let me wear one of my Sunday dresses, because I was thinking of the Great Visitor I was entertaining.

Dressed once more, I ran to my room and sat in my little chair quietly, seriously, respectfully, using my best manners; and I began to make acts of love—many acts of love—to my God. I embraced myself, because in me I embraced Jesus. A thousand promises of love and fidelity I made to Him in my childish language, and I knew that Jesus understood me very well—much better than my father or mother.

I felt so vividly within me the presence of my God, though in a manner much different from the way I perceived my New Friend. It was as if I myself were the good Jesus—He, my Divine Guest, listened to me without being bored. And I, without hearing His holy voice, listened attentively and lovingly to what Jesus wished from His little servant: that I never, never commit even one sin, so that He, Jesus, might never be separated from me—not even once, not even for one moment!

Then getting up from the chair, I knelt down and made a little cross with my two index fingers. This I kissed in my childish simplicity and said with the most firm resolution: "O good and beloved Jesus, I swear to Thee, my Lord, that I do not want ever to commit any sin." This was the first and only oath that I ever took in the world. Perhaps I did not understand the immense obligation that I assumed. I cannot say, but I do know this much: I made this oath, moved by a great desire never to offend the good God. Until today I kept this oath as a secret in my heart. I never revealed it to any one. I took this oath while Jesus was within me and my New Friend was at my side.

And this is the moment when I reveal my secret. Jesus, the good Jesus, accepted and guarded in His most Sacred Heart this oath of a weak creature; and through His grace He took care that this oath was never broken, even to this date.

*   *   *

O MY GOD, please continue to take care of Thy little spouse. Enclose in Thy most Sacred Heart until my last breath this oath which I made to Thee with such great love and sincerity.

In my simple intelligence, I often understood the exact opposite of the explanations which the good Sisters gave us in our religion classes. Thus it happened that I conceived the erroneous idea that when we received Our Lord in Holy Communion the Real Presence of Our Lord Jesus Christ remained in us until we should commit the first sin after the reception of this Holy Communion.* This conviction, although

---

*After the reception of Holy Communion, Jesus remains within us, Body and Blood, Soul and Divinity, until the corruption of the sacred species, i.e., until the accidents of the bread and wine have been changed by the digestive functions of the body.

wrong, was of immense benefit to me, because it filled me with a greater horror of sin, since I was convinced that only one sin would cause me to lose my Divine Guest. And I wanted never to lose Jesus. I would suffer the loss of everything, even of my father and mother, who were everything to me, rather than lose Jesus.

Chapter 3

Learning How to Say
the Rosary

UP TO the time of my First Communion, I had little knowledge of the holy Mother of Jesus. However, after the incident of the white roses and the effective intercession of Our Lady in obtaining permission for my First Holy Communion, I began to love her more—much more—through a great grace of the good God. The *Hail Mary* was, of course, the first prayer I learned in honor of Our Lady. Then Mother Raphael taught me the following prayer:

Remember, O tender Mother,
   that I belong to thee!
O Blessed Lady, guard me and
   defend me,
As thy very own property!

I always recited this short prayer in the morning and at night, up to the time I entered the convent. I had learned also to make little sacrifices in honor of Our Lady. I was filled with great joy when Mother Raphael taught us how to say the holy Rosary. I returned home radiant with joy. The *Key of Heaven* prayer book which Mother Raphael had given to me contained all the usual prayers. I knew by heart the *Our Father*, the *Hail Mary*, the *Creed*, the *Hail Holy Queen*; but I did not know what I should be thinking of during the mysteries of the Rosary. However, the *Key of Heaven* would teach me. "How wonderful," I thought after our lesson in religion. "Today I shall say the Rosary at home, and I shall also teach Cyprian how to say it." Cyprian was a poor old man in the beggars' asylum which was located near our house.

When I arrived home that day, I was in a hurry to do everything. I wanted Acácia to give me my bath as soon as possible and, following this, my father to help me with my studies. (My dear father always helped me in my studies, and with great patience, until I was nine or ten years old.) The reason for my hurry was that I wanted to say the Rosary alone, for the first time. But neither my father nor Acácia was at my disposal when I got home. Father had not yet come from the barracks, and Acácia would not leave the kitchen until my father arrived. I resolved, therefore, to begin the Rosary.

I fetched the *Key of Heaven* and placed myself at the foot of the big bureau in order to pray before the little plaque of Our Lady. Only then did I realize with great confusion that I did not have a rosary. However, I remembered that Acácia had a big necklace of blue beads which looked like a rosary. I resolved to use them.

I ran to fetch this necklace. The only thing lacking was a cross. I did not have one, but Our Lady knew this and it did not seem to be too important. My New Friend was there, and I felt him observing all my movements and thoughts. Likewise, Our Lord.

I knew that all holy pictures, rosaries and medals should be blessed. So I reasoned thus: Acácia's necklace is not something holy, and therefore it is not blessed. So, kneeling down, with great devotion I took the necklace and placed it in the palm of one hand, while with the other hand I made the Sign of the Cross over it, saying in all sincerity: "I bless thee in the name of the Father and of the Son and of the Holy Spirit. Amen."

Thus I recited my first Rosary. I am very certain even today that Our Lady accepted lovingly my first recital of her holy Rosary on that necklace of blue beads, which I used in my childish simplicity. My New Friend and Our Lord remained with me during this Rosary, and they did nothing to oppose me.

Having finished the Rosary, I treated the necklace with great care and respect. I thought to myself: "From now on, Acácia cannot adorn herself with this necklace, because I have blessed it. I will ask her to give me the necklace, and I will give her the money I have in my Noah's ark bank. However, Acácia in her goodness would not accept the money. She gave me the necklace as a gift and accepted only a small package of chocolate cigars, which I had bought for one cruzeiro.

Toward the close of that year, when we were celebrating the ending of classes, I received as a prize a little purse of blue and white satin containing a beautiful small white rosary, which the good Mother said was already blessed. This was the first rosary I ever owned. And on the very next day, the beginning of our vacation from school, I went to the asylum to teach my friend, the paralyzed man, how to say the Rosary. For about two months I had been saying the Rosary on the beads of the necklace.

Twice I had attempted to go to the asylum to teach the poor old man through the medium of the necklace, and each time my New Friend had hindered me. But once I received the beautiful white rosary, my New Friend did not oppose me any longer. Instead, he accompanied me to the asylum.

*   *   *

MY good Jesus, most holy Virgin, and most faithful Guardian Angel, certainly in your tender love you forgave the great ignorance of your little servant and only regarded the good will and ardent love of your simple, ignorant Cecy.

"My Friend Cyprian"

I believe that I should now narrate something about my good friend, the paralyzed man of the asylum. From the time that we arrived in Jaguarão from Santa Vitória, we lived in a house which was situated in front of the beggars' asylum. This asylum was a big one-story house, divided into a large number of rooms. Each room had a window facing the street. The asylum provided shelter, but nothing else, for the destitute poor.

In one of the rooms that had a window facing our house there lived a poor old paralyzed man who could move only his head and left hand. We in our house, and all the passers-by, could see this poor old man from dawn to darkness, for his bed was alongside the window, which was always open. He was propped up by pillows in the bed. My mother, who felt very sorry for him, took it upon herself to bring him his meals every day.

One day I accompanied Acácia to the asylum. Before this I had seen the old man only from a distance through the windows of our house, and I had noted his head, white as cotton, and his long white beard. Now, however, I got a close-up view of him. Acácia would not allow me to enter the room. As I waited at the door, a few feet away from his bed, I observed him attentively. Now his long beard, white as cotton, reminded me of our picture of the Most Blessed Trinity, in which my beloved heavenly Father was represented also as having a long beard, white as cotton. In that picture my heavenly Father never appeared angry with me. Even after I had committed some fault, He still seemed to regard me with kindness and love.

And what else did I notice about the poor paralyzed man? A crucifix of white metal, larger than the palm of my hand, rested on his chest. It was fastened around his neck by a cord. I thought to myself: "I already like this poor old man very much. I shall take care of him so that his soul and his heart may become as white as snow for the good Jesus." After Acácia had placed his meal on a little table, she spoke a few words to him. Then taking me by the hand she returned with me to the house. During the rest of the day I thought often about this poor sick man. That night, upon retiring, I prayed to my New Friend:

"My New Friend, tomorrow I wish to visit the poor old sick man and to speak with him about our heavenly Father. I ask you to go with me. I do not want to go with Acácia, because she is always in a hurry to leave."

It happened that we had a two-day holiday from school. So, early in the morning, after Acácia had returned from the asylum, I ran to the window of the room from which I could see the old man. There he was, as always,

propped up in his bed. I left the house, crossed
the street, and walked toward his window. With
some difficulty I climbed up to the window ledge
and sat upon it. The old man looked at me
and seemed to be surprised by my visiting him
through the window. I thought he was frightened, so I said to him: "Don't be afraid. I am
the same little girl who came here yesterday
with Acácia. I live next door."

At this the old man looked very happy. I asked
him to show me his beautiful cross. Taking it
from around his neck, he handed it to me. And
then, without forgetting even one point, I
repeated in its entirety that first holy lesson
which I had received two years before from my
beloved Dona Mimosa. The old man listened
and listened to me, without interrupting me
once. When I finished the lesson, he began to
cry, just as "little Dédé" had cried in the arms
of Dona Mimosa. I told him to kiss the figure
of Our Lord on his beautiful crucifix. This he
did, and then he hung it once more around
his neck.

I promised him that I would return on the
following morning and that I would bring with
me the china plaque of the Holy Mother of Jesus,
so that he could see it. My New Friend was with
me all this time, but he did not sit on the window ledge as I did. I never perceived my New
Friend seated. I believe that he was always standing at my side, because oftentimes, when I was

still very small, I lifted up my head to try to see his holy face. However, I never did see it.

On the following day I kept my promise. After breakfast that morning, which was a holiday, I took the plaque of Our Lady and went across the street, seating myself once more at the sick man's window. I showed him the image of Our Lady and told him she was the Mother of Jesus. Then I taught him how to say the *Hail Mary*. However, it took many days before the poor old man learned to say it by heart. Every day I would seat myself on the window ledge of his room, usually in the afternoon after returning from school at four o'clock. I never missed my visits, as I knew these made the old man very happy. On rainy or very cold days in the wintertime, when I was not allowed out on the street, I would watch my poor friend from the parlor window of our house. I loved this poor old man with all the affection of my heart, and I was certain that he liked me very much.

In this way the months sped by. Cyprian finally learned to say the *Hail Mary*, the *Our Father*, the short prayer to one's Guardian Angel, and the *Memorare* to Our Lady. It was about this time that I made my First Communion. At the end of the school year, as I have said, I received as a prize a beautiful white rosary, the first that I ever owned. As soon as possible, I ran over to the asylum to show it to my beloved protégé and to teach him how to say the Rosary of Our

Lady. This time my New Friend did not object, as he had done when I wished to teach the old man how to say the Rosary using the beads of the blue necklace. Cyprian soon learned how to say the *Creed*, the *Our Father*, the *Hail Marys* and the *Glory Be to the Father* on the various beads of the rosary. But he did not learn the mysteries for the very good reason that his little "catechist" did not know them. So I would read from the prayer book—not very well, as I still had difficulty in reading—and the poor old man would pray on the beads.

Very often, when my mother looked out the window, she would see me visiting the old man. Then she would summon me home and I would be punished. On those occasions I would leave my rosary with Cyprian and say to him: "Cyprian, this evening when the street lights are lit, begin to pray on the beads, while I, in my house, will read from the *Key of Heaven* prayer book what you should be thinking. Our Lady too knows everything, hears everything, and sees everything, just as her Son Jesus does." On the following day I would fetch my rosary. This happened many times.

As I am writing now, I think of another great favor that I received from Our Lord. In my contact with this unfortunate poor man, uncared for and afflicted with various diseases, I could easily have caught one of these diseases were it not for the special protection of the good God. I remember numerous occasions when I kissed the figure of the Crucified on the old man's crucifix immediately after he had done the same thing.

*　　　*　　　*

O MY good God, I give Thee thanks for Thy paternal protection of my body and soul. O my God, may what I am writing here serve solely to glorify Thee!

Cyprian's Baptism*

One day when I was at home reading the mysteries of the Rosary and Cyprian was praying on the white beads of my little rosary, my mind was suddenly filled with the realization of a dreadful thought that had vaguely disturbed me for some time: "Mother Raphael said in class that whoever is not baptized cannot enter Heaven." And as big tears began to run down my cheeks, I thought: "My poor friend Cyprian, then, will not be able to go to Heaven to see Our Lord and Our Lady, because he is not baptized."

As was my custom in such mental problems (and also when I committed some fault), I lifted my head, trying to see the holy face of my New Friend. He was there beside me, for without see-

---

*It is evident that Cecy had not yet learned at this time, or did not yet understand, that lay persons may baptize only in case of necessity.

ing him with my eyes, I perceived him; and without hearing his holy voice with my ears, I heard him and understood him more perfectly than I could understand my father, my mother, Mother Raphael or Acácia. Soon my tears stopped as a new thought rolled the clouds away from my soul: "I can baptize Cyprian. I know how to do this. Mother Raphael taught us. I know very well how to baptize." Then and there I went through the act of baptizing. I was sorry it was nighttime and I wished that the following day would quickly arrive, so that I could bring to my dear Cyprian the good news of his approaching Baptism.

On the following day I went to school. But in the afternoon, when I was free of all duties, I ran to the asylum, climbed on the window sill and told Cyprian what I intended to do for him. The good old man was very, very docile and obedient to his little catechist. He was always ready and happy to do anything that I asked him. When I told him that in order to enter Heaven and see Jesus with His holy Mother it was necessary to be baptized, for I had learned this from Mother Raphael—I added that I was able to baptize him—so great was the joy of the old man that big tears began to flow from those eyes marked by long years of suffering. I tried to console him as well as I could. I told him that if he would not cry any more I would bring him on the following day a holy card of Our Lady which Sister Eugene had given me.

Then the old man, very childlike, pulled from beneath the pillow a big, red-striped handkerchief and dried his tears. I began my "instruction" in preparation for holy Baptism by saying: "Mr. Cyprian, Mother Raphael told us that Baptism washes away all the sins of grown-up people. Now, you are a grown-up person. Your soul will become as white as mine was on the day of my First Communion." At this the old man began to cry once more. His tears affected me so much and filled me with such compassion that I used every means to console him and also to keep myself from crying with him. Finally, I said to him: "If you continue to cry, you will not get the holy card." Hearing this, the poor old man once again pulled out the big red-striped handkerchief.

I marked his Baptism for a Sunday, and told him: "Sunday is the Lord's Day, the day on which I go to Mass. Then I shall be wearing a nice dress for your Baptism. On any other day but Sunday Acácia would not allow me to wear one of my good dresses or my best shoes." I do not remember the day or the month of his Baptism. I know only that it was a Sunday.

I prepared well for this holy festival of my poor friend. The guests would be my New Friend and myself. On the day before the Baptism, which would be a Saturday, I should have school only in the morning. I went to fetch my Noah's ark bank. I needed only a few more pennies to be able to buy the enticing black drink sold in the Girls' Shop and costing twelve cruzeiros. As I thought of this, my selfish desires became very strong and I was reluctant to empty the bank. However, because my New Friend was there, I lifted up my head to try to see his holy face. And without seeing it, I perceived it. I realized at once that he disapproved of my reluctance, for his holy face regarded me with sadness.

So, resolutely, I emptied into my lap the ten shining cruzeiros that my father had saved for me. At that moment it seemed to me that nothing in the world would make me change my mind. Even if someone had said to me what I then most wanted to hear: "Keep your money; save it up, and you will soon be able to buy that enticing black beverage!" I would not have changed my mind, because my New Friend had a greater influence over my will than the whole world. Therefore, without saying anything to anybody, not even to Acácia, I put the money in the little purse that I had received some time before and went off to my favorite candy shop.

My New Friend was not sad any more. On the way home, as I held the lovely package of bonbons, chocolate cigars, and chocolate bars covered with silver paper, I felt just as happy as on the day when, in company with Acácia, I had crossed the river, carrying the beautiful bouquet of white roses for Our Lady. More than once I lifted up my head, trying to see the holy face of my New Friend, who was no longer sad, and I said to him: "All these are for Cyprian. I will not take even one chocolate cigar for myself. With these Cyprian will be able to celebrate his Baptism on Sunday."

When I arrived home, no one saw me entering, and no one had missed me. I did everything naturally, as I was never accustomed to act secretly. However, thanks to the Lord God, no one ever found out about these things. Then I began to ask myself: "Is there anything else lacking?" I myself would be wearing my best clothes—my new dress, my best shoes and stockings, a pretty ribbon for my hair, and so on. Then I remembered that Cyprian had nothing new or beautiful for his Baptism. This made me sad for a moment, until I solved the problem very quickly in the following way: Cyprian was always in bed. Therefore, tomorrow I would bring him one of my father's nice new shirts, with starched collar and cuffs, and also a knitted undershirt, together with some eau de cologne to put on his hands and face.

In my child's simplicity and eagerness I brought all these to Cyprian on the following day. When I related this incident just recently in the convent, I was asked if I had sought and received my father's permission to give away his shirt and undershirt. Only then did I realize that I had not proceeded properly. Perhaps it was because I was accustomed to obtain anything I wanted from my father, and I knew very well that he would give me anything possible, especially anything that I needed for the poor old man. I always considered that whatever belonged to my father belonged to me also.

Finally everything was ready. After my bath, I ran over to the asylum with the two big packages. I did not hide from anybody, yet nobody saw me. On account of the packages, I had great difficulty climbing up to the window sill. Through the window I handed the two packages to Cyprian, and then I told him what he had to do, saying: "Tomorrow you must put on this beautiful new shirt, and underneath it this new, white undershirt. In this little bottle you will find perfumed water to put on your hands and face tomorrow, so that you will smell really nice."

At these words, the poor old man began to cry. In order to console him, I gave him the package of chocolates to keep for the morrow. Then I was filled with wonderment, because he cried still more. I did not realize that he was crying from gratitude and deep emotion.

So I said to him, "Don't cry, Mr. Cyprian, as we must say some prayers in preparation for tomorrow." Only then did he stop. I said with him all the prayers that I knew by heart: the *Creed*, the *Our Father*, the *Hail Mary*, the *Hail Holy Queen*, the prayer to the Angel Guardian, the *Memorare* and the Act of Contrition. Before taking my departure I remembered Sister Irene's advice to us on the day of our first Confession; so I passed this on to Cyprian, telling him to be very good from now on and not to be looking out on the street. The poor old man promised to be good.

On the following day, which was a Sunday, I went to holy Mass and read nearly all the prayers in the *Key of Heaven* prayer book for Cyprian. Certainly Our Lord must have smiled at me. When I returned from Mass, I asked Acácia to let me continue wearing my new dress. Since Acácia was always my good friend, she let me have my way.

I was so filled with the thought of the great act that I was about to perform that my heart beat violently. I fetched the little pitcher that my mother had bought for my trips to the dairy farm. Although it was clean, having been in the china closet, I washed it once again. Then I filled it with water from the well and began to walk over to the asylum. I wanted to run, but I could not do this with a pitcher full of water. I placed the pitcher on the window sill, where I also perched.

I had expected to find Cyprian looking beautiful in his new shirt and undershirt, but alas, there he was, wearing his old shirt. I had not remembered that the poor old man was unable to dress himself and that he had no one to help him, but I now accepted this unforeseen fact. I looked at my New Friend. He was satisfied; so I would be able to baptize Cyprian, even though he was wearing his old shirt, which, however, was quite clean. Once more I repeated with him the Act of Contrition. Both of us, the old man and myself, were deeply conscious of the great Sacrament that he was about to receive and I was about to confer. My New Friend was there also. I told Cyprian to incline his white head, and this he did. Then, kneeling on the window sill and with my heart pounding strongly, I poured the whole of that pitcher of water over the head of the old man, making sure that the scalp was really wet. At the same time I said, just as Mother Raphael had taught us, "I baptize thee in the name of the Father, and of the Son, and of the Holy Ghost."

Afterward I said to the old man, "From now on you are to go by the name of Joseph in honor of St. Joseph." I gave him this name because he reminded me of St. Joseph by reason of his long white beard. The poor old man began to cry again, and placing his one good hand on the large crucifix that hung from his neck, he said: "My good God! My good God! My good God!" I remember that scene perfectly.

I was filled with a great happiness, just as on the day of my First Communion. And my New Friend was very, very pleased with me. As I bade good-by to the old man, I said to him: "Your soul and your heart are as white as my soul was on the day of my First Communion." I always used this comparison when I wanted to say that something was very white.

But alas! Little did I realize what would happen on the following day! I know now that for the poor old man it meant attaining the highest happiness. But as a child I felt only the great sorrow of losing my poor, sick friend. On the day after his Baptism, Acácia, as was her custom, brought breakfast over to the old man. We were still at the breakfast table when Acácia returned in a few moments, crying out in great sadness to my mother: "Dona Antoninha, Mr. Cyprian died this morning." My mother was greatly saddened by the news.

And I—how did I feel? Only the good God could know the great sorrow that filled my heart. I wept over the loss of my poor friend, and for a long time I missed him. My mother would not allow me to go to the asylum to see his body. I saw nothing of the funeral. I do not know what kind of funeral they gave him. And when I returned from school at midday, I did not even look toward the window of his room. For many days afterward that window was closed, until another old man came to occupy it. Over a long period, with sad remembrances, I said the Rosary on my white beads for the repose of Cyprian's soul.

*　　　*　　　*

Good Mr. Cyprian, I am certain that you are

enjoying now the possession of your God and mine, and that you know now your most holy Mother in Heaven. Your little catechist is still living in this wretched world, but for a long time you have been one of our Divine Saviour's guests at His great banquet. You will come with my Jesus.

The Rosary in the Arbor

After the death of the good Mr. Cyprian I ran into a difficulty. I had been accustomed to recite the Rosary with him. For a long time after his death I said the Rosary for him on my beads, but I did not say it with the same facility as when I had prayed with him. When I recited it alone and in a low voice, it took me twice or even three times as long to say, because I was distracted very easily and was always starting the *Hail Marys* all over again. How wonderful it would be, I thought, if I always had someone to recite the Rosary with me, just like Mr. Cyprian! Acácia knew how to say the Rosary, but she always told me that she had no time. My sister Dilsa said the Rosary with me a few times, but she never had the patience to finish it. She would always end up by saying, "Now you say the rest of the Rosary, as I am tired."

So I usually had to say the Rosary alone, beginning it over and over again; and many times the street lights were lit before I had finished. I was unhappy whenever I had not said my daily Rosary, because I felt that the Mother of Jesus had not received my prayer to her on that day. If I had not been able to recite the Rosary during the daytime, I would not be able to sleep at night, because I would feel so upset. Therefore, on such nights, when I was already in bed, I would sit up in the bed as soon as Acácia had put out the light and say the Rosary. Only then could I go to sleep.

I thought and thought how I could solve this difficulty, which I found such a burden. Finally, I betook myself to Isaura, a little friend who lived next door to us. Isaura was very good; so, telling her of my difficulties, I invited her to recite the Rosary with me. She agreed to do so, saying: "Very well, but let us go to the arbor, and then no one can laugh at us." I did not understand the reason given for going to the arbor, but then I did not try to understand it. So I went with her. Isaura recited the whole Rosary with me on that day, and during the next few days she showed her good will. But one afternoon she said to me in the middle of the Rosary the same words that my sister Dilsa had said: "Oh! but I'm tired. I cannot pray any more; let's play instead!" As I could not remain alone in the arbor, because it was not on our property, I had to start playing with Isaura. Later that evening I finished the Rosary in bed. From that day on, only very rarely did Isaura accompany me in the recitation of the holy Rosary.

The Box of Bonbons

One day I received from Captain Teixeira (pronounced Tay-shay´ra) a very pretty little box of bonbons. The cover had an elephant mounted on a bicycle, the wheels of which really revolved. I was radiant with happiness. I thought that nothing in the world could make me part with that beautiful little box filled with bonbons. But at the very moment when I was filled with admiration for that pretty box, suddenly the thought came to me: "I ought to give this box of bonbons to Isaura, without even tasting one, because she accompanied me in reciting the Rosary."

This idea came so quickly that I put it aside, and it was followed just as rapidly by another, namely: "I shall not give even one bonbon to Isaura, because she does not want to pray with me any more." And then I felt and perceived (I do not know how to express myself) my New Friend looking at me sadly and seriously, although I did not see him with my bodily eyes. As was my custom in such instances, I lifted up my head to try to see his holy face. I was puzzled: My New Friend wanted me to give this box of bonbons to Isaura. Only now do I understand that there was a conflict between my will to obey my New Friend and my selfish desires. But as always, my New Friend conquered, and my wretched, ugly selfishness was overcome.

So I took the pretty little box, and with the speed of an arrow I ran to Isaura's house. There, with great joy, I handed her the box of bonbons, saying: "This is for you, because you wished to help me in saying the Rosary." On that day and for some days afterward, Isaura said the Rosary with me. But later on she gave up accompanying me in its recitation.

I could never find anybody else among my young friends who wished to recite the Rosary with me. The years passed but my difficulty remained. However, through a grace obtained for me by the holy Mother of Jesus I always said her holy Rosary every day. When I finally entered the convent, to my great joy I encountered another postulant, Sister Alphonse, who always accompanied me in the recitation of the holy Rosary whenever it was possible for her to do so. We began this holy custom when I said to her one day: "Gloria, I have so much difficulty in reciting the Rosary alone; would you like to say it with me?" And she consented to do so.

When I became a novice, this difficulty passed away. I was told never to repeat a *Hail Mary*. Thanks be to God and Our Blessed Lady, I was cured of this scruple. After this, on innumerable occasions, I said the Rosary for Mr. Cyprian, for my sister Dilsa, for Isaura and Sister Alphonse. This was a small tribute of gratitude that I paid to them. Only in Heaven will those generous souls know of the great benefit they bestowed on me and of the happiness and consolation they gave me when they helped me recite the holy Rosary.

Chapter 4

The Year of My Confirmation

IN THE year 1907 I received the holy Sacrament of Confirmation. On that day, as on the days of my first Confession and First Communion, I did not want to play in the street lest I stain my soul by some small sin. The house in which we lived at that time had a large orchard. It was my great delight to carry my little chair out to the orchard and seat myself beneath a big pear tree. There I would read the little book that I had won in school, and which was entitled *Stories for Children*. On the day of my Confirmation, instead of going out on the street I seated myself beneath the pear tree. I thought that would be a good place to preserve my soul and my heart free from sin. The day before I had gone to Confession, and that morning I had received Holy Communion. It was on such days especially that I felt a great fear of committing sin. While I sat in my little chair, keeping as holy as possible, I paged through my book. Suddenly my attention was drawn to a long lane of ants, some going backward, others forward, rapidly and without interruption. I then seated myself on the ground in order to get a closer look at them.

And at that moment, in my great ignorance, I really desired to be one of those little ants. If my New Friend should have asked me why I entertained such a strange desire, I would have answered without hesitation: "Those little ants are better creatures than I am, because they do not commit sin; they never hammer any thorns into the Sacred Heart of the good Jesus. But I would commit many sins were it not for the constant protection of my New Friend and the divine presence of Our Lord in my heart!"

From that day forward I felt a great love for all little creatures and animals, and I desired to be one of them. This idea remained in my head until I was about ten or eleven years old. I am sure Our Lord did not judge strictly this strange desire of mine, for He well knew how simple and foolish His little friend was. Whenever it happened that I accidentally crushed one of these little insects, I experienced a great sorrow.

However, I came to realize later on different occasions that not all animals were good-tempered. At such times I would excuse them, saying to myself: "Those animals do not have a New Friend like mine to warn them against committing sin."

Major Reveilleau, our neighbor, had a big watchdog named Bilac. On one occasion Bilac broke into our yard and killed two rabbits. We ourselves had a pair of bulldogs that my father had received as a present. They were called Veneza and Nero. Nero was very good-tempered, but oftentimes Veneza was just the opposite. When Acácia gave them their food, Veneza would eat more than she should. Then, if Nero approached to eat what was left, Veneza would bare her teeth, growl and bark; and poor Nero would have to keep at a safe distance while self-ish Veneza stood guard over the remains of the food. "What a bad dog she is!" I thought. "She cannot eat any more, yet she will not allow Nero to eat."

These incidents and many others which I witnessed were considered by me in my simplicity as the sins of the animals. When I came to realize that animals also were capable of selfish and cruel acts, I gave up completely my peculiar desire to be one of them.

*   *   *

AND NOW, O my New Friend, in order to glorify our good God and to pay tribute to thee, my holy and faithful Protector and Guardian Angel, I shall narrate how on many occasions I was on the point of committing sin but did not sin, because thou wert watching over thy little friend most faithfully, and thy protecting hand hindered me from falling.

The Open Basket of Sugar-Cane Cakes

One afternoon during the summertime Acácia took us for a walk in the country. There were a number of children from the neighborhood in the group, among whom was one girl whom we shall call Nilce. We went toward the racecourse. When we arrived there, Acácia organized foot races. As was her custom, she had brought with her a basket of "good things," and she said to us: "Whoever wins will receive a prize." Then she showed us what was in the basket. How our hearts leaped with joy! For it was full of sugar-cane cakes. Nilce ran in all the races, but she lost every time. I lost also, for as soon as I began running I got a pain in my side.

After the races Acácia said to us: "Those who won will receive two pieces. The others will receive only one. Before I give them out, let us visit Dona Manuela." The latter was a very good old Negress who lived in a small house nearby. Then we went over to visit Dona Manuela. When we arrived there, Acácia left the basket of sugar-cane cakes outside the door of the house while we went inside. Dona Manuela took us out into her little garden while she picked some flowers for us.

Then Nilce said to me: "Acácia is very bad. The sugar-cane cakes are from your house, but now she is going to give you only one piece. Let us go back to the basket and take two pieces for ourselves." It seemed to me that Nilce was right, and I thought that I had the right to take all the cakes if I cared to do so. So we turned aside from the group and returned to the basket. We opened it, and our mouths watered at the tempting sight. "Two is nothing," said I to Nilce. "Take four pieces for yourself and I'll take four." Nilce helped herself and put the pieces of cake in her pocket. Then I bent over to do the same, but at that very moment I felt on my shoulder the sweet, tender, meek and friendly hand of my Guardian Angel. Ah, holy hand, so well known to me! I stood up straight and lifted my head to try to see the holy face of my New Friend, who was looking at me so sadly. I saw him, not with my bodily eyes, not as one sees other persons, but I saw him in another manner.

In the meanwhile Nilce urged me on, saying, "Be quick, for the others are coming." She began to eat hurriedly all the cakes that she had taken. She had made the last one disappear when Acácia returned with the other children to find the basket open. I was standing beside it, but Nilce was not to be seen. Acácia was very angry and grabbed me by the hand, saying: "Little deceiver, you would take these cakes! But now all the other children will receive their pieces, while you can watch them eat."

This punishment was not too hard for me, because I felt truly sorry, sincerely repentant for the ugly sin that I realized I had been about to commit. In my imagination I saw the thorn with which I nearly wounded the sacred head of Our Lord. I had looked at my New Friend many times since his holy warning at the basket. He was sad only when I was on the point of sinning. Now he was not sad any more. His great, immense goodness aroused similar sentiments in my heart and made my repentance much greater.

We returned to the racecourse, where Acácia divided the cakes. I remained a little apart from the group, as if I were ashamed of having committed an ugly action. No one, not even Acácia, knew of Nilce's part in this little drama. She was with the other girls. When I saw that Acácia was also going to give her some of the cakes, a wave of indignation and rebellion swept over me, as I thought: "Acácia is not right. Nilce took the cakes and ate them, and now Acácia is going to give her some more." Of course, in my anger I forgot that Acácia, who was always very just, did not know what Nilce had done.

Indignant and angry as I was, I was determined to accuse Nilce, because she was laughing at me with the others. However, as I started to move rapidly, once more I felt the holy hand of my New Friend hindering me from going any farther and accusing Nilce. Once again his holy face was sad. My repentance was again instantaneous and so bitter to me that I began to cry. Acácia naturally thought that I was crying on account of the punishment which I had received. Feeling sorry for me, she called me to her.

I looked at my New Friend and he was pleased once more. My emotion was so great that I ran to Acácia. Throwing myself into her arms, I clasped her around the neck and wept until I was exhausted. Then Acácia gave me the rest of the cakes, but I did not even taste them. For a long time afterward—I think for about two years—I did not taste even a crumb of the delicious sugar-cane cakes that I liked so much. This is the first time that I have ever narrated this incident.

The Doll which Lost Its Eyes

In a raffle I won a big doll. It was so big that I could barely carry it. On account of this my mother did not allow me to play with it, as she feared that I would break it. This doll was always on the sofa in the parlor, and I regarded it as a great treasure. It could open and shut its eyes, and if you pulled a little cord suspended from its shoulders, it would say, "Dadda, Mamma." Acácia always went with me to the parlor when I was going to play with the doll, so that I could handle it under her watchful eyes.

Now my little sister Adayl was very small and very mischievous. One day Adayl found the door of the parlor open; so, entering, she walked over to the sofa and pulled the doll down toward her. I do not know why it did not break, but a little later she was found with the doll. When I returned from the school, Conceição said to me: "Go into the parlor and take a look at your doll. Adayl was playing with it." I ran immediately to the parlor, and there I found the doll stretched out on the sofa. Her lovely blue eyes with their long eyelashes were gone; and in their place were two ugly holes. Adayl had pushed the eyes in with her fingers.

When I was confronted with that tragic scene, for one moment I remained as if turned to stone. Then immediately came the reaction. In a wave of violent indignation, the tears burst from my eyes; and at the same time I said to myself: "I'll find that little wretch, bring her here, show her what she did to my doll, and then I'll box her ears." So I ran out in search of Adayl.

At the end of the corridor I saw Adayl creeping on all fours like a cat. Crying out in my anger, I had not reached the door when I felt the holy hand of my New Friend (I do not know whether I can speak thus) preventing me from continuing. I lifted up my head, as was my custom, to perceive his holy face, which was regarding me with sorrow. Then, as if I clearly heard his voice, I was made to understand: "Adayl committed a bad deed without realizing it, and I want to punish her because I am angry." I was moved by this realization. I began to cry

more, not now out of anger but because once
again I had saddened my New Friend; and I
knew that if he was sad the good Jesus was sad
also on account of me.

But now his holy face did not appear to be
sad any more. I was filled with joy, much greater
than any I ever received from looking at the
doll.

*   *   *

MY beloved New Friend, once again I thank thee;
and at this moment I realize that thou didst stop
me from performing a low act of vengeance. And
Thou, most merciful Jesus—I thank Thee for the
great grace Thou didst give me of always attending
to the voice of the most faithful Friend that I have
in this world after Thee and Thy most holy Mother.

Chapter 5

Some Incidents of
the Year 1908

AT THE beginning of the school year of 1908
all the children were very much interested
in collecting holy cards. Each child had a beautiful little box in which to keep them. There
was great rivalry to see who would have the
most beautiful box and the greatest number of
holy cards. At that time all the children placed
a high value on a holy card, and when they
received one in the classroom from the Sisters,
they were filled with happiness. Sometimes the
girls would bring their boxes of holy cards to
the school, and during recreation they would
show them to the others. Then the girls would
exchange different holy cards.

One day Lucy, who sat beside me in class,
brought to school her beautiful little box filled
with holy cards. In the classroom she showed
them to us. During recreation we spoke about
the beautiful collection that Lucy had. Then we
returned to class. During the last period Lucy
left the classroom to take her piano lesson.
While she was absent, I noticed Lucy's other
neighbor putting the box of holy cards in her

pocket. I saw this action of my companion, but since I was busy with my books I thought nothing of it, and soon I forgot all about it. When school was over, we went home.

We returned that afternoon, and during recreation I noticed all my classmates talking together. Lucy was telling them about her missing box of holy cards, and she was accusing me of the theft. Then I remembered what had happened in the classroom that morning and I understood the action of my companion: she had stolen the box of holy cards. In the schoolyard a large group of girls surrounded Lucy in one corner, sympathizing with her, while I was left alone in the opposite corner, humiliated, suffering bitterly from the false accusation, feeling keenly the indignant stares that were directed at me.

Suddenly and instantaneously there arose within me a strong feeling of indignation joined with the resolution to fight back in blameless self-defense. In the middle of the group was the real culprit and she also was looking at me. So far the knowledge of the theft had not reached the ears of the Sisters. Carried along by my indignation, I decided I would tell Mother Raphael the name of my companion who had taken Lucy's holy cards. I would add that I had seen her, but that it was she who had accused *me* of the theft.

Yet I did not take one step forward to carry out my resolution, for I immediately felt my

New Friend opposing my plan of self-defense. I turned to look at his holy face, and I perceived that it was sad. I did not understand why he opposed my desire to defend myself. Only now do I understand his reason, which I think was this: He did not want me to defend myself by accusing another, even though the accusation was true. Once more my New Friend triumphed over my self-love. At the end of recreation all of us returned to class, while I remained under the heavy weight of that shame, since all my classmates thought I had committed that ugly sin. But the holy face of my Friend was joyful-looking once more. This was my only consolation, so great was my humiliation and shame.

When I returned home after school, I did not relate this story to anyone in the house. Such was my custom, although I had no special reason for being silent. Not even my sisters knew of this false accusation. Some time afterward Lucy found her box of holy cards in her desk. Then I thought: "Certainly the Guardian Angel of the girl who stole them must have commanded her to return the box of holy cards, so that she would be able to make a good Confession and become once more a friend of the good Jesus."

At the Merry-Go-Round

One afternoon upon leaving school practically all the pupils of Sister Eugene found themselves with some coins. We had brought the money for our Sodality meeting, but there had been no meeting. One of the girls had an idea: "Why not go to the square and ride on the merry-go-round, and afterward buy fruit salad at the refreshment stand?"

The idea was approved by a unanimous "Let's go!" from all the girls. The square was some distance from the school and still farther from my house. As we walked along I suddenly remembered: "It will be late when I get home and my mother will not like it. Besides, I do not know how to get home alone." (That day my sisters had no class in the afternoon.) Laila, one of my companions, answered my objections, saying, "All of us will get home late, so we can say that we were at the school." Everyone agreed to this, including myself, since I was delighted with the thought of going to the square, riding on the merry-go-round and eating fruit salad at the refreshment stand. So we went.

We rode on the merry-go-round after having to wait a little while, since it was filled with children. Then we went to the refreshment stand, where we regaled ourselves with fruit salad. It had been half-past three in the afternoon when we left the school. It was now getting late; so

Laila and another girl accompanied me to the corner where Mr. Delelis lived. From there I knew the way home.

Up to this point everything went very smoothly, and I was walking home happily and peacefully with my pack of books under my arm. Then suddenly a thought came to trouble me: I was going to tell my mother that I had been at school all afternoon, so that she would not punish me. For the first time in my short life of eight years I was going to lie. Because this was so, I had not at once realized that I was going to tell a lie, and would therefore be committing a sin. Through my young head surged reasons for and against this lie. The wily tempter reminded me: "But all the girls are going to give this excuse. Why cannot you do the same?"

As my conscience was trying to solve this problem, I recalled the sad story that Sister Irene had told us two years before, when giving us instructions for our First Communion: how a little boy had been sent to Purgatory because he had lied. At this point my New Friend, who had accompanied me to the square without opposing me, made me lift up my head to try to discover his holy face. I perceived it perfectly and sensibly, yet without seeing it. His holy face was very sad, because I wished to drive a thorn into the sacred head of Jesus. Immediately my willingness to lie to my mother changed, and I resolved to tell her where I really had been.

Then I began running home, and I arrived there with my heart pounding. Acácia had already gone looking for me. I told my mother frankly where I had been. She did not like it, and so she scolded me. But my New Friend was happy once more, and I, too, felt happy. Many times during my childhood I was tempted to lie, but my salvation was always the thought of the punishment of the poor little boy who was sent to Purgatory because he had lied. However, a much deeper impression was made on me by the warning of my New Friend that a lie wounded the sacred head of the good Jesus, who loved me so much, and whom, by His grace, I already loved very much.

The Circus

In the year 1908 a circus company came to Jaguarão. The circus pitched its big tent on a piece of land set aside for this purpose which was only two streets from our house. On our way to school every day we passed the circus. One night my father took us to see the performance. Afterward my father said that the circus acts were not very good and that the entrance fee would be too high even if it were only a penny. However, my opinion was altogether different from that of my father and mother. I thought the circus the most beautiful thing in the world, and I would gladly have gone to see it every night.

I was enchanted by the different acts—for example, when the little dogs climbed to the top of a high rope ladder and from there jumped into a wide sheet held extended by the attendants. I was thrilled to see the little girl walking on a big ball, and to see an older girl hanging by her feet from a trapeze. But what delighted me most of all was the ugly clown with his face covered with powder. He kept turning somersaults so quickly that he seemed to be a great big ball rolling around.

I considered those performers to be completely different from ordinary people, and in my admiration I placed them on a very high plane, for I did not understand how they could do all those wonderful things. My admiration extended even to the circus children of my own size. Each day when I was going to or returning from school, I felt attracted to the big circus. I always wanted to stop and look through the big gate, and my sisters had to pull me by the hand to get me away from there.

I thought: "How wonderful it would be if my mother allowed me to play with those circus children! Then they would perform their acts for me, and I would get a close-up view of the clown." But I knew very well that my mother would not allow me to go there and that Acácia would not take me. So I resolved: "On the day that my sisters do not have school in the afternoon, I shall be returning alone, and then

I can enter the circus grounds." Everything happened according to my plan.

When I was returning alone from school at half-past three in the afternoon, I went to the circus gate. There were many men, women and children there, but I thought that these were not the performers because the latter would always be dressed in their beautiful costumes. I made my way to one of the men who was standing at the gate and smoking a big pipe, and I said to him: "Mister, are you the owner of the circus?" He answered "Yes"; so I continued: "I liked the clown so much and also the children of my own size that I came to play with them." The man laughed, and taking me by the hand, he said: "Very well, come and I shall take you to them."

I had not yet passed through the entrance of the big gate when I was prevented from going any farther by my New Friend, in such a way that I felt pulled in two different directions. The circus owner was pulling me by my right hand, while my New Friend pulled me by my left hand, in which I was carrying my school books. I do not know what my New Friend did to the man. I know only that the man freed me suddenly and violently, saying, "Get out of here!"

Only then did I get frightened and run away from the place. When I reached the corner near our house, I looked at my New Friend. Since his face was not sad, I forgot the whole incident quickly. But from that day I was afraid of the big circus and I never went there again. To this day I do not know why my New Friend prevented me from entering, and did it with so much energy. Recalling that incident now, I realize that once again my New Friend saved me from some great evil, to which I had exposed myself unwittingly.

*   *   *

O MY holy and most faithful Friend, once more I return thanks to thee, and I praise my God and thy fidelity.

The Lost Brooch

The incident which I am now about to relate happened on the birthday of Major Reveilleau. That evening the Major gave a banquet and a dance, to which my father took me. Both celebrations were held in the house of Captain Barcelos, and from there everyone went to the house of the Major. I was only eight years old at the time. So, when we arrived at the house of Captain Barcelos, my father left me with the women while he went to join the group of men.

When everyone left for the Major's house, I walked along very quietly. I remember well how I was dressed and that I wore a brooch bearing my name. This was in fashion at the time.

Soon I noticed that my brooch had fallen off. I left the sidewalk and began to look for it along the gutter. In the meanwhile, the big group of men and women was passing by without paying any attention to me as I was bent over, looking for the brooch on the ground. Finally, the whole group disappeared in the distance without missing me while I was engrossed in my search.

Having looked for the brooch for some time without finding it, I gave up the search and only then did I notice that I was alone in the deserted and dark street. From afar I heard the low murmuring of voices growing fainter and fainter. Frightened and feeling lost, I ran this way and that without knowing which direction I should take. I had run thus about two blocks when I was forced to stop from exhaustion and a strong pain in my side. I rested against a wall on the street corner.

Up to this point I had not met anybody. But a few minutes afterward I perceived that someone was coming in my direction from the end of the street. Thinking it was my father coming to look for me, I wanted to run to meet him; but my New Friend, who up to now had been very reserved, prevented me from proceeding, just as he had done in the incident with the circus owner. As was my custom, I obeyed my New Friend without the slightest resistance, and I returned to the place where I had been leaning against the wall. Now, however, I was very calm and without fear. I awaited tranquilly the approach of the person who was making his way toward me. Soon I could distinguish him. It was not my father, for my father would not be walking like that. It was a man wearing a smock, who came staggering along from one side of the street to the other, stumbling at every step.

I was not afraid. My New Friend was there with me, but this time he was not at my side as usual. He was in front of me. I perceived him without seeing him with my eyes. Nevertheless I kept very quiet, hardly breathing. The man would pass by me, and my New Friend wanted me to keep very quiet. Soon the man came staggering up to my place, muttering words I could not understand. He passed directly in front of me. His smock brushed against my legs, yet he did not see me.

After the man had passed I went with my New Friend to the house of Major Reveilleau, who was our neighbor. There was a band playing in front of the house, and the street was filled with groups of curious onlookers. Nobody paid any attention to me. I looked for my father. When I found him, I perceived that he had not even noticed my absence. Only now do I realize that the man in the street was certainly drunk. Once again my most faithful New Friend saved me from an evil of which I am ignorant.

Chapter 6

Holy Week of the Year 1908

ONLY in the year 1908 did I begin to understand the real meaning of Holy Week. Sister Irene told us the tragic story of the Passion of our Divine Saviour. To emphasize her words she showed us large pictures of different scenes of the bitter sufferings of the innocent Jesus. As Sister Irene related each sorrowful event, my soul was pierced with sorrow and remorse, and I was filled with the desire to love more and more my good Jesus and to detest with greater horror wicked sin, the sole cause of the sufferings and death of my God.

The picture representing the crowning with thorns made such a deep impression on me that this scene remained engraved on my soul during all my childhood and girlhood. As if it were only yesterday, I remember well how Sister Irene showed us that sorrowful picture and then drove home the lesson by saying to us: "Even today each one of you, just like those evil soldiers, can hammer a crown of thorns into the sacred head of Jesus. In what way do we do this?"

My sister Dilsa answered, "By committing sins

willingly." At these words a great weight was lifted from my soul. Many times I had been bad and had committed sins, but always without willing to do so.* Whenever I had been tempted to commit a sin, my New Friend had prevented me from doing so. Certainly Sister Irene must have spoken to us of Lent in general; yet I understood nothing about that holy season except Holy Week, which filled my mind. I waited anxiously for that week, so that I might be able to "help Jesus, and keep Him from suffering so much." Thus I thought in my childlike simplicity.

Holy Week finally arrived. I went to Holy Mass in the school chapel and we received blessed palms. During all of the Mass I thought and thought what would be the best way for me to keep Jesus from suffering so much. Now I had a special love for my sister Dilsa. When we arrived home I called her to the foot of the large bureau on which stood the crucifix and the plaque of our Blessed Mother, and I confided my desire to her by asking: "Dilsa, do you also wish to help Jesus during Holy Week?" She answered, "I already know what I am going to do and what I am going to say to Jesus on Good Friday."

On Monday my little sister went out and returned with a length of crepe. She explained

---

*Sister Maria Antonia here seems to refer to semi-deliberate sins and faults.

to me that during Holy Week our Blessed Lady and all the saints were sad and in mourning. On account of this the pictures were turned around and covered with crepe. So Dilsa covered all our holy pictures with crepe, including the crucifix and the plaque of Our Lady.

During that Holy Week my young soul felt a great sorrow for the good Jesus and His holy Mother. On Holy Thursday we made our paschal Communion with the other students. It was after this Holy Communion that I discovered what I should do to keep Jesus from suffering so much. I knew then what I was going to say to Jesus on Good Friday at three o'clock, in union with my sister Dilsa.

After Mass we went home. That night I could not sleep, so great was the sorrow I felt for my Divine Saviour. My very soul was filled with that picture which Sister Irene had shown us representing Jesus in agony in the Garden of Gethsemani. I carried Jesus in my heart, and I felt Him suffering the bitter torments of His Passion. I clasped Him to my breast. In my anxious desire to help Him, although I felt so helpless, I did not want to wait until the following day, until three o'clock the afternoon of Good Friday. I arose in the darkness and placed my hands over my heart, because I knew Jesus was resting there, or rather that Jesus was suffering there. Then I went to the foot of the big bureau, whispering to Jesus in my simple, child's way:

"O poor Jesus, how sorry I feel for Thee! I do not want all those sins to cause Thee such great sorrow. Please hide Thyself in my little heart. Then wicked men will not know that Thou art with me, and I shall tell no one. But I know that it is also necessary for wicked men to stop committing sin; so I ask Thee, dear Jesus, to take away all the sins of men and to hide those sins also in me."

I prayed thus because Sister Irene had explained to us that Jesus had suffered for the sins of the whole world, including those of each one of us. In my eight-year-old mind I thought I could lighten Jesus' burden by taking the heavy burden of those sins from His shoulders and hiding them in me. At least by my good will I certainly gave a little consolation to my Divine Saviour on that night of sorrow. I remember that I myself was convinced that I had consoled Jesus. So in peace and contentment, I returned to bed, certain that Jesus was suffering less than before.

On the next day, Good Friday, we went to church. My great preoccupation was to hide Jesus and the sins of men. That afternoon we spent at home. When it was nearly three o'clock, my sister Dilsa called me and said: "Do you know yet what you are going to ask Jesus at three o'clock?" I had not told Dilsa what I had done the night before, because I wanted to repeat the same thing at three o'clock on Good Friday. My sister and I waited at the foot of the big bureau until the clock should strike the sacred hour.

I cannot explain what I felt in my soul at that moment. I felt and perceived vividly the Divine Presence in my heart, and I had the sorrowful fear that if Jesus should die in me I would lose Him until Easter Sunday. Moved deeply by this sorrowful fear, I exclaimed: "O good Jesus, Thou must not die in me; not even for three days must Thou die." I could not bear the thought of being without the presence of Jesus or of my New Friend. Then the clock struck three. I repeated the prayer I had said the night before. How great was my joy when [I realized that] Jesus had not died in my heart, but willed to hide Himself there and [to hide there] also the sins of the world!

A few moments afterward my sister Dilsa said to me with tears in her eyes: "I told Jesus that I preferred to die before another Holy Week rather than commit a sin deliberately." Only now, amid tears of emotion, do I realize that the dying Jesus granted my little sister the grace she had asked of Him. Dilsa did not live to see another Holy Week. She died in less than a year, on January 14, 1909, which fell on a Thursday. The same clock was striking three in the afternoon as my little sister breathed her last in the same spot where she had asked Jesus for that special grace, namely, at the foot of the

big bureau upon which stood the crucifix and
the plaque of our Blessed Mother. Three days
before her death the doctor had ordered her
changed to that room.

*   *   *

O GOOD JESUS, forgive me for never thanking
Thee for this grace that Thou didst grant to my little sister! Only now, as I recall this series of events,
do I realize everything. O my God, how much I am
indebted to Thee! My Jesus, forgive my ingratitude!

Chapter 7

The Street Urchin

IN ORDER to show the greatness of God's mercy toward me, His little creature, and to reveal the fidelity and constant protection of my New Friend, I shall now relate certain experiences that will prove how little was my intelligence and how lacking I was in cleverness. In these experiences God and my New Friend could have given me their special help, but they did not do so. They allowed me to act according to my own limited intelligence, so that I might realize, at least today, how much I owe to my God. To Him I owe everything.

One afternoon I was playing on the street with Inácia, who was two or three years older than I. This was in the year 1910, when I was ten years old. We were no longer living in front of the asylum. As we skipped rope along the street, we finally arrived at the corner near Inácia's house and stopped there. As we looked around, we saw a boy coming toward us from the opposite direction. He was about fourteen or fifteen years old, and was one of those poor boys whom people call street urchins. I knew him by sight, as every day he passed our house.

He delivered meat and vegetables to the houses.

Inácia said to me: "Do you see that boy? If you say 'shrimp' to him, he turns into a shrimp; and if you say 'crocodile,' he turns into a crocodile." The boy passed us, but [I knew that] soon he would return with the meat and vegetables. Then I said to Inácia: "But does he turn back again into a boy?" "Certainly," she said, "for the other boys shout these names at him all the time. When he returns this way, shout 'shrimp' and 'crocodile' at him, and you will see."

"I will shout only 'shrimp,'" said I, "for that is very small. I will not say 'crocodile,' for that is too big and dangerous. I would be afraid, and besides the poor boy would have to suffer, going through such a change."

"Oh, he would not suffer anything," said Inácia, "and he does not mind it anyway."

We waited until the boy returned a few moments afterward. Then Inácia said to me: "I will wait here at the door of the house while you go to the corner. Otherwise the change will not take place."

Excited at the wonderful thought of seeing a boy changed into an animal, I went to the corner. As the boy was passing by me, I said to him as he was right in front of me: "Shrimp!" Great was my disappointment when the boy, instead of turning into a shrimp, said to me very angrily: "You will pay for this and pay well."

In the meanwhile Inácia was hiding behind the yard gate and was laughing so much that she could not stop. I did not understand at the time why she was laughing, but of course she had known that the boy became very angry whenever he was called names.

Some days afterward, as I was going to school alone one afternoon, I met the same boy on the street. We recognized each other, and he said to me, "Now you will see who is a shrimp." Saying this, he hit me on the arm and then ran away. I was not accustomed to such rough tactics; so, instead of continuing on to school, I returned home weeping and related the whole story to my mother. Then my mother became angry, not with me but with the boy, and she said: "He should have complained to me and should not have hit you. This cannot be."

We were now neighbors of the regimental commander, and every Thursday there was an open-air band concert in front of his house. One Thursday I saw the boy who had hit me, sitting with other boys, listening to the music. I pointed him out to my mother, who told Abelino to bring him into the house. There in the corridor Abelino spanked him with a slipper. I could hear him yelling from where I was on the veranda, and Acácia said to me: "Abelino is giving the boy a beating because he hit you." I was just about to answer: "Very good," when my New Friend prevented me. Then I sought

to look at his holy face, which was sad. At that
my soul was filled with a great sorrow for the
poor boy. I ran out to the corridor to make
Abelino stop beating the boy, but he had already
freed him.

I returned to the veranda, but my soul was
now overwhelmed with such sorrow that I could
not hold back the tears. As Acácia had left the
veranda, I wept for a long time in sorrow and
repentance. I asked forgiveness of the good
Jesus and of my New Friend. I confessed my
fault, saying: "That poor boy received a beating
because I told my mother he had hit me. But
he gave me only a slight tap that did not hurt,
while Abelino is very strong and he must have
hurt the boy very much."

I wished to go to Confession at that moment,
but it was Thursday and I would have to wait
until Saturday. This filled my soul with a new
sorrow. I thought: if I could only go to Padre
Godofredo now! But there were many difficulties in the way. It was getting dark, and soon
the street lights would be lit. Acácia was occupied in the kitchen and Conceição was setting
the table. If I went I should have to go alone.
Should I do so? I looked at my New Friend,
and what was my joy to see that his holy face
was not sad anymore. The good Jesus had already
forgiven me, and my New Friend had done the
same. Then I would wait until Saturday to con-
fess everything to Padre Godofredo.

But if peace had returned to my soul, a great sorrow and feeling of repentance remained. If that boy had appeared before me then, I would have given him a thousand proofs of my new feeling toward him. In my Noah's ark money box there was only one coin. I resolved to buy chocolate cigars with it and to give them to the boy on the following day. Immediately I went to the candy store and returned with ten chocolate cigars. On the following day I waited anxiously for the boy to pass by our house, but he did not come. I watched for him on the two following days, but he did not pass by. Naturally he was afraid to go by our house after that beating. In my childish mind I imagined a thousand other reasons except the right one. I even thought that Abelino might have beaten him so much that he had become sick, and had perhaps died. This thought frightened and oppressed me.

Some weeks passed by, and one day when I was outside I saw the boy passing down the street. Without hesitation I ran toward him and said: "I have something for you. Please wait until I fetch it. I am very sorry that Abelino punished you." The boy looked at me strangely, but he did not refuse to wait for me. I did not have any more chocolate cigars, but I did have some money in the Noah's ark. I took it quickly and ran back to the street, fearing that he might have fled. But he was there when I returned. I gave him everything, the money and also the Noah's ark. He was so happy, and off he went with the money and the little bank. As for myself I felt the sweetest peace in my heart. I remained at the corner with my New Friend, watching the boy until he had disappeared.

Chapter 8

"My Automobile"

IN THE year 1910 my father was transferred to the military garrison of the Upper Uruguay River while we children remained in Jaguarão with Mother. This separation from my father was a great sorrow to me. In the previous year death had taken our little sister Dilsa, and now I was to be separated for a time from my father, whom I loved above everybody else, except Jesus, His most holy Mother, and my New Friend.

We went down to the dock to bid farewell to my father, and we went on board ship. When the ship's siren blew the first warning signal, I felt such sorrow at being separated from my beloved father that I felt I was going to die. I threw my arms around his neck, weeping convulsively. And when the sad wailing notes of the second whistle filled the air with sadness and loneliness, I should certainly have died of anguish if I had not felt the holy hand of my New Friend disengage me gently from my father. I did not resist my New Friend. My eyes dried as if by a charm. I looked at my father and at my New Friend who, in his most sweet voice, whispered words that were heard, not by my

ears but by my heart and soul. He whispered:
"The good Jesus wills this."

If at that moment I could have remained with
my father I would not have done so for anything in this world. For I loved the good Jesus
and my New Friend much more than my father.
Therefore, when the ship blew the final whistle, I descended to the dock without any further tears. From there, as the ship was loosed
from its moorings, I waved my handkerchief at
my father, from whom, a few minutes before,
it had seemed impossible for me to separate.

After he had spent some months at his new
station, my father obtained permission to return
on furlough to Jaguarão. As a present he brought
me a beautiful little automobile, in which I
could pedal around the streets. This was a source
of the greatest pleasure for me. Every day, after
returning from school and finishing my studies, I would take out my automobile and ride
from one end of the square to the other. The
stone pavement, however, was never intended
for smooth driving. In many places the flag-
stones were broken; so I had to make many
detours.

One Sunday, Zita, a little friend of mine, came
to visit me. She had her tricycle with her and
she said to me: "Let's go down to the main
square. There it is perfect for riding. The streets
are long and wide and paved with mosaic." On
Sunday and Thursday afternoons it was the cus-

tom for the people of the town to congregate
in this main square. A band or orchestra played
music in the bandstand erected in the center
of the square. A continuous procession of young
girls, women and children passed in parade
around the outskirts of the square, while in the
center men and youths seated themselves at the
tables of the outdoor bar or stood in groups
in front of the refreshment stand. The merry-
go-round was always filled with children.

My mother gave us permission and Acácia
went with us. This was the first time I had taken
part in these open-air assemblies. When we
arrived at the square, I pedaled my little automobile around and around. The wheels glided
smoothly over the mosaic pavement. There were
no bumps, no detours, no stops. I returned
home delighted beyond measure. I made
arrangements with Zita to return to that square
every Sunday afternoon. We kept our agree-
ment, and two or three Sundays afterward there
was a continuous stream of tricycles being driven around the outside of the square.

In the year 1909 Padre Godofredo Evers
became confessor to the students at our school.
He was one of the professors at the boys' *ginásio*, which was called the Ginásio Espírito Santo.
This school fronted on the main square of the
town. One Saturday in Confession this good
priest said to me, "Cecy, I do not like the idea
of your spending Sunday afternoons riding

around the main square. Do you understand?"

I understood perfectly, but during the week I forgot about the Padre not liking my trips to the square. When Sunday afternoon arrived, I made my way as usual to the square in my little automobile, for this was my greatest source of pleasure. On that Sunday, however, I saw my confessor seated on a balcony that jutted out from a window of the school, but he was half-hidden by the balustrade. He also saw and recognized me, for he waved to me. On the following Saturday he spoke to me once more about my trips to the square. But when Sunday came and my friends arrived to accompany me on their tricycles to the square, I completely forgot about my confessor's counsel. My New Friend had not yet opposed my going; so off I went in a transport of joy with my young friends.

We found the square filled with people, and I saw Padre Godofredo seated in the same place, praying or reading a book. He noticed me, for each time I passed by the place where he sat he looked at me. He smiled at my evident happiness, and his two warnings against coming to the square never even entered my head. However, I was soon to remember them.

Suddenly a quarrel broke out at the foot of the statue of Liberty which was erected in the center of the square. Immediately everyone ran toward the scene of the quarrel. I lost sight of Acácia, for she had been standing on the opposite side of the square while we drove round and round. At the sound of the quarrel our group of children on tricycles stopped, and everyone shouted: "Let's go and see what's up!" Some of the children then began running across the square toward the statue.

Filled with excitement, I began to get out of my little automobile in order to run after the others. But I did not take even one step before once again I felt the holy hand of my New Friend upon my shoulder. My New Friend held me gently but firmly, so that I could not move. My eyes sought his holy face as I turned my head to the right. All this happened rapidly. At this time I was in front of the *ginásio* gate. I now perceived that the holy face of my New Friend was sad. At the same time I saw Padre Godofredo running down the many steps of the *ginásio* entrance and crossing the street toward me with long, rapid steps.

I had understood nothing of what all this meant. In my astonishment I had remained immovable. When Padre Godofredo reached me, he said in a tone of gentle severity: "Go home immediately, and never come back here again. Otherwise you will make the good Jesus sad."

Only then did I realize the seriousness of the counsel that my confessor had given me. It was not just a simple wish on his part; it was an order given by the good Jesus, and I had not obeyed it. A feeling of sincere and bitter repentance filled my soul, and I began to cry, saying at the same time to the holy priest: "Padre, I do not know where Acácia is and I cannot find my way home alone. Will you take me home?" Padre Godofredo looked at me for a moment, while perhaps his generous apostolic soul was overcoming a natural feeling of human respect. Then he took me by one hand, and with the other pulled the automobile. He left me at the corner near my house. In parting he said to me: "Go now, with the blessing of the good Jesus and in the protection of your Guardian Angel!"

"Thank you very much, Padre," I replied, "I shall never again be disobedient."

I had gone only a few steps when I heard Acácia calling me. I waited for her. When she had caught up with me, I said in my naïve frankness: "I wanted to go home, and since I did not see you, I asked Padre Godofredo to take me home." I was astonished when I saw the amazed look on Acácia's face. Opening her eyes widely, she exclaimed in indignant tones: "Well, my fine lady, you don't have much respect for anybody, do you? Do you think Padre Godofredo is your servant?"

This observation filled me with greater remorse for my disobedience. Acácia told the story to my mother, who repeated it to my father. On the following day my father wrote a note to Padre Godofredo, and I, accompanied by Acácia, delivered it. I remember that on several nights during that week I wept tears of repentance on my pillow, because I had saddened the good Jesus and my New Friend. However, the holy face of my New Friend was not sad any more, but such goodness to me only filled me with greater repentance. On the following Saturday I confessed my disobedience to Padre Godofredo and promised never again to go to the main square on Thursday or Sunday afternoons. With the help of God's holy grace I kept this promise faithfully. On the following Sunday, instead of going to the square at the usual hour, my little automobile remained in the house while I went to the parish church to fulfill the penance imposed on me by Padre Godofredo. There, before the altar of our Blessed Lady, I said the Rosary for all the children of Jaguarão.

Chapter 9

Confirmation Sponsor
for the First Time

IN THE year 1911 I acted as sponsor in Confirmation for the first time. My little godchild was the daughter of our laundress. Her name was Elizabeth and she was a little girl about five years of age. She was to be confirmed when the Bishop made his visitation to Jaguarão. This bishop was the same one who had confirmed me. (In Brazil the custom exists of confirming children any time after their Baptism.) I was filled with joy at the thought of being godmother, and I anxiously awaited the day of Confirmation. I was filled with complete happiness and I thought often of the serious obligation that I was about to assume.

On the appointed day I left early with Elizabeth for the parish church. I knew well how to get there. Besides, Acácia could not go with us. Padre Domingos, the pastor, would give me all the information I needed. I had in my purse the stipend I was to offer. This was the small sum of three cruzeiros. We made our way to the church without any difficulty. Sponsor and godchild were both radiant with happiness.

As we came in front of the church I saw a great crowd of people. I was pleased with this sight, as it meant that the Bishop was already there. Elizabeth, however, did not share this feeling with me. When I told her that the Bishop was already there, thinking to make her more happy, Elizabeth began to weep a torrent of tears, punctuated by loud yells. She was afraid of the Bishop. I made a thousand promises to her in an effort to quiet her. I cradled her in my arms, but she only wept and cried the louder. I told her that the Bishop was a saint, that he was very good and kind, that he was very fond of children. But it was all of no avail. The nearer we came to the church, the more Elizabeth wept.

This took away all my joy. "Very well," I said to Elizabeth, "we shall not go to see the Bishop. I myself can confirm you *in case of necessity*,* just as I baptized my friend Cyprian." This was another wrong opinion that I entertained at the age of eleven years. I thought, wrongly, that Confirmation could be administered under the same conditions as Baptism. However, I do not think that Our Lord judged too strictly this

---

*The ordinary minister of Confirmation is the Bishop alone. The extraordinary minister is a priest to whom his faculty has been given by common law or by a special indult. It is impossible for a layman to administer the Sacrament of Confirmation.

great ignorance of His little friend and this presumption to try to take the place of the Bishop.

I seated myself with Elizabeth on one of the benches in the square in front of the church, and I began to give her some "notions" about the holy Sacrament of Confirmation. I trust that my New Friend did not allow me to teach any heresy to that little soul. He was there and his holy face was not sad, for I had observed him more than once. Three or four times I tried to get Elizabeth to enter the church with me to see the Bishop; but as soon as I mentioned this, she began to weep loudly once more. I waited for a long time, until the Bishop and all the people left the church. Then Elizabeth quieted down.

We went into the church, which was now empty. I went directly to the altar of Our Lady, whose image appealed so much to my very heart. This was a beautiful statue of natural height representing the Immaculate Conception. Elizabeth and I knelt in front of this statue and we prayed. First, we asked forgiveness for all our past sins. Then we promised Our Lord and Our Lady that we would never more offend them by sin. We ended by reciting the Act of Contrition. Elizabeth was now very docile, and with her hands joined she repeated everything.

Leaving the altar of Our Lady, we went to the baptistery which was on the right. I was disappointed at not finding baptismal water in the big marble font. Then we went to the holy water font near the entrance. My heart was now beating rapidly because of the great emotion that I felt. I knelt down with Elizabeth, and once more I recited with her the Act of Contrition and all the prayers that I knew by heart. Then, standing up, I filled my hand with holy water. I knelt down once again, and with the water I traced a cross on the forehead of Elizabeth, while at the same time I said with all the fervor of my child's soul: "I confirm thee in the name of the Father and of the Son and of the Holy Spirit. Amen."

I was now filled with happiness. In my simple faith my new "godchild" seemed more beautiful to me now than before. Perhaps it was my imagination; or more likely it was the result of my strong faith, by which I considered her little soul as being now without the slightest stain of sin. In my great happiness I said to her: "Your soul is now as white and dazzling as mine was on the day of my First Communion." This was my usual comparison.

I do not know the reason why, but all through my life I preserved vividly in my mind the keen recollection of the whiteness of my soul on the day of my First Communion. Only in recent years, beginning in 1935, did I lose in my inmost being that which was for me the sum of my delights, namely, the vivid realization that I had within me Him who is Incomparable Brightness Itself, the God of my soul.

*   *   *

O JESUS, since that time when Thou didst begin to hide Thyself from me, I have been oppressed with the terrible and sorrowful feeling of a soul in gloom and obscurity, of a soul weighed down by the thick darkness of sin.

But I must continue my story about Elizabeth. I believed that Elizabeth was now confirmed; so I led her to the first bench, from where I pointed out to her the tabernacle, or "the little holy house" in which Jesus lived. Then we left the church. I suddenly remembered that I had three cruzeiros in my purse, which I needed no longer. With this money I could buy bonbons for my "godchild." We went to a candy shop, and the three cruzeiros were soon exchanged for a pretty package of bonbons, which I handed to Elizabeth.

Leaving the shop, we began to walk home. We had not gone far, however, when the thought suddenly came into my head: "I have bought bonbons with holy money." All money that was destined for the Church or for the poor I considered holy money. I now judged that I should have placed those three cruzeiros in the poor box at the door of the church. I was bothered very much by this thought. What could I do to remedy the situation? Should I bring the package of bonbons back to the owner of the shop and ask him to give me back the very same cruzeiros that I had given him in payment? Then I could give three other cruzeiros to Elizabeth. But I realized also that I did not have another penny in my purse.

I did not know what to do. In my limited intelligence I was convinced that I should deposit in the offering box of the church the very same money which my father had given me for the Confirmation stipend. Finally, I decided to go back to the candy shop. There, in all sincerity and with tears rolling down my cheeks, I explained my problem to the owner. Great was my surprise when I saw Mr. Carvalho begin to smile and then to laugh heartily. Taking the package of bonbons that I had returned to him, he handed it to me, saying: "I am going to make you a present of these bonbons."

Then, going to the cash drawer, he gave me back the very same money with which I had paid him. Radiant with happiness once more, I thanked the good shopkeeper. Elizabeth and I ran to the church, where we deposited the three cruzeiros in the offering box. I now felt great happiness and consolation. This incident taught me a lesson that I never forgot during the rest of my life. From that day forward I never used any money, no matter how small was the sum, without inquiring first where it came

from and for what purpose it was to be used.
Later on Elizabeth was actually confirmed by
the Bishop, and I was her sponsor in reality.

Chapter 10

Learning to Make Sacrifices

IN THE year 1911, when my father returned home on vacation to Jaguarão, he brought me a beautiful gift. This was a toy car which contained the figure of a country girl driving a flock of geese in front of her. When one pulled the car, the girl clapped her hands and the geese flapped their wings. I got immense pleasure out of this toy. Acácia gave me a ball of twine. I tied the twine to the little car, which I left at the corner of our house. Then I walked to the other end of the street while I unwound the whole ball of twine. Standing there, I began to wind the ball of twine once more, and thus I pulled the little car all the way from my house to where I was standing. This delighted me so much that every afternoon I was to be found on the sidewalk, pulling the car from one end of the street to the other with the ball of twine.

One afternoon I noticed that each time I passed from one corner to the other I was accompanied by a poor Negro boy who was about seven or eight years old. With intense interest he watched me play with the toy car, and each time that it fell over along the way, he ran to lift it up. I began to feel a certain type of satisfaction on seeing that "my beautiful little car" was the cause of such admiration to this little Negro boy. Two or three days afterward the little boy was there as usual, watching me and accompanying me. Finally he offered me an orange, saying: "Would you like to exchange this orange for your little car?"

This proposal caught me by surprise and I answered rather proudly: "My car is of much more value than a whole sack of those oranges. Besides, I have as many oranges as I want." The little boy did not answer. However, I had no sooner said those words than I felt the holy hand of my New Friend on my head. He wished to tell me something. I listened to his voice speaking to my soul. What I heard puzzled me. I should give up my little car. The beautiful toy which my father had given me and which I liked so much I should give to the poor little Negro. Immediately the thought came to my mind: "I cannot give it to him, because my father gave it to me." But this thought was succeeded at once by another: "The good Jesus wishes me to give it to him." I looked at my New Friend. His holy face was not sad, but it was grave, as if he were awaiting my decision.

Resolutely I looked at the little boy, who was holding the orange in his hand and watching the car like one in ecstasy. I said to him: "Very well, I'll give it to you. I'll give the car to you."

Winding the ball of twine quickly, I pulled the car toward me and gave it to the boy. For one instant he remained hesitating, as if he doubted the fact of the gift. Finally I convinced him and he accepted it. Once more I looked at my New Friend. His holy face was grave no longer but filled with that "sweetness" which made me so happy, for it told me that Jesus was satisfied with His little friend.

I did not know then which one of us was the more happy at that moment, the Negro boy or myself. But now when recalling that incident, I realize that I was the more happy—that I was incomparably more happy. Yet at that time my New Friend reminded me that I had spoken harshly to that little boy. I wept over this sin, and on Saturday I confessed it to Padre God-ofredo. On his advice I brought, the next Sunday, the toy I liked most to Padre Domingos for the poor children in his catechism class. Padre Domingos had asked for "old toys." So at first I began to pick out dolls that had lost an arm or a leg, the cup without a handle, the cock that did not crow any more, the faded ball. As I was putting these in a cardboard box, I felt my New Friend placing his holy hand on my head.

I stopped to listen to his most sweet voice. He reminded me of the beautiful tea set of twelve pieces that Colonel Ferreira brought me from Rio. Without playing with that tea set even once, I placed it with the other toys and took them all to Padre Domingos. For the "sweetness" of the holy face of my New Friend was to my young soul more precious than the most costly toys in the world.

*   *   *

Padre Godofredo was the director of the Sodality of the Children of Mary. One Saturday at the beginning of the school year in 1912, he told me in Confession that he greatly desired to see me received into the Sodality of the Children of Mary during that year. There was one impediment: I was not old enough, or at least I lacked the necessary intellectual capacity. But said he, "Let us begin today to pray and to make little sacrifices in order to obtain this great grace from Our Lady on the eighth of December."

I left the confessional radiant with happiness, as if I had already received the beautiful medal with its pretty ribbon. This illusion of mine continued for some days, and I did not even begin to make little sacrifices in honor of Our Lady, as my confessor had told me. Finally I began to think seriously of the priest's words. As regards praying, I knew what I would do. Of all the prayers that I knew there was none better or more powerful than the Rosary. I never let a day pass without saying the Rosary, even to the present time, thanks to our Blessed Lady. The difficulty lay in the sacrifices. I did not know what sacrifice I should make in order to please the Mother of Heaven. I did make some sacrifices, but I felt that these were not what Our Lady wanted.

Here I must relate my special weakness: I had a great liking for sweets, for cake and candy, especially for chocolate. To speak sincerely, I was gluttonous. Acácia knew my "weak spot," and she gave me whatever I desired. Perhaps it was a big piece of jellied marmalade, or an eggnog with cinnamon, or a handful of raisins, or anything that came to hand. When there was no candy or cake, or when Acácia was too busy, I would go to the kitchen myself and fill a paper bag with lumps of sugar. This was a good substitute for candy.

One afternoon I filled a paper bag with lumps of sugar. As I took one and began to raise it to my mouth, I felt the holy hand of my New Friend preventing me from completing the movement. Looking up at his holy face, I saw there that serious look which I knew so well. Without understanding the reason why he hindered my arm, I emptied the bag into the big sugar can. The holy face of my New Friend soon lost its seriousness, which was succeeded by that incomparable look of "sweetness" that gave me all my joy, all my happiness. However, I did not understand why my New Friend had prevented me from eating the sugar.

Some days passed by, and one afternoon I was on the veranda studying my lessons, when Acácia came out from the kitchen with a dish of roasted fruit for me. This made me very happy, and I showed my pleasure by embracing Acácia. Acácia placed the dish on the table and then went inside. I took a piece of fruit and tried to raise it to my mouth, but I found my arm hindered once more by my New Friend. I looked at his holy face, which was grave. Then I understood the meaning of it all: I had such a great liking for sweets and everything with sugar. I must give up these things. This was to be my little sacrifice in honor of Our Lady. This was the sacrifice the Mother of Heaven wanted in exchange for the beautiful medal with its blue ribbon.

In order not to make this chapter too long, I shall say only that from that day forward (the middle of March, 1912) until December 8 of the same year, I never tasted the smallest piece of sugar or any kind of sweets. Padre Godofredo said to me: "Take sugar only in your coffee." I followed this rule. I know that the most holy Virgin accepted this little sacrifice of her child, because on December 8 she rewarded me with the beautiful medal of the Children of Mary on its blue ribbon.

On the day that I received this medal, Padre Godofredo gave me a holy card of Our Lady and said to me: "Cecy, today you can eat as many sweets as you wish, and Our Lady will be very happy." When I returned home, I found that the ever good and thoughtful Acácia had not forgotten me. She surprised me with what she called "a little mouthful." When I went out on the veranda, at the place where I usually studied, I found a plate of prunes stuffed with coconut. Great was my surprise, then, to discover that I had lost completely my gluttonous tastes.

*   *   *

IT is to thee, most holy Virgin, and also to thee, my most faithful New Friend, that I owe everything. Amen.

Chapter 11

Angelic Censorship

URING the school vacation from December, 1911, to March, 1912, my father resolved to send me to Santa Vitória do Palmar. He was advised to do this by our family doctor, who wanted me to benefit from bathing in the salt water of the ocean. I was to leave soon after the closing of school, in the second half of December. I was to live with the family of a lady who was a friend of my parents. We shall call this lady Dona Nayá. She had two daughters boarding in our school in Jaguarão. It was a great trial for me to be separated from our family. More than once, when my mother and Acácia were packing my traveling cases, I saw them weeping. This made me feel the coming separation much more.

On the day of departure my father accompanied me to the dock. There I and the two daughters of Dona Nayá were handed over to the care of a certain colonel. My leavetaking at home had been very sorrowful. The steamer was to depart at two o'clock in the afternoon. Early that morning Acácia called me to go to Holy Mass, during which I received Holy Commu-

nion. Thus I would not have to travel alone.
Jesus and My New Friend would accompany me.
For many days before the journey I was fearful
lest my New Friend would not be able to accompany me because of some weighty reason that
would detain him. Naturally, however, this did
not happen. Padre Godofredo gave me a holy
card bearing a picture of a Guardian Angel. On
this card was written the beautiful little prayer
which I knew by heart and which I recited every
morning and night:

> Holy Angel of God,
> My devoted guardian,
> The divine mercy has confided me
>   to thy care;
> Always watch over me,
> Rule and govern me,
> And be ever a light to
>   my footsteps. Amen.

We had a pleasant journey and arrived at
Santa Victória on the following morning. Dona
Nayá and her husband were at the dock to meet
us, and they surrounded me with every care,
love and devotion. Yet, I greatly missed my parents, my sisters and Acácia. Within two weeks I
fell sick with a high fever, and were it not for
the continuous presence of my Jesus and my
New Friend, I believe that I would not have
been able to withstand the hard separation.

After some time I grew better. Then my friends began to make preparations to go to their house by the ocean. These preparations were cut short when they received the news that their house had burned down. Changing their plans, they resolved to spend the vacation at their big ranch.

The pleasant and active life of the ranch little by little made me forget my homesickness, and within a short while I began to feel perfectly at home. There was much to divert us. We could watch horse races, or we could go horseback riding, or we could go driving in a horse and carriage. One afternoon, amid great enthusiasm, the family planned a picnic and swimming at the nearby waterfall. The neighboring families were invited.

The Extended Wings

With much shouting and laughter the group set out. Some were on horseback; some were in the carriage; others were in the small wagon. Dona Nayá took me with her in the carriage. I was filled with happiness. When we arrived at the waterfall, I stood in awe and admiration as I looked upon it for the first time. From on high the water came tumbling down, roaring and foaming as it hit the enormous rocks at its base. Then it settled down to flow calmly across a soft bed of sand.

The men set to work to cut down branches.

From these they fashioned some rough shelters. In these the groups undressed and put on their bathing suits. Dona Nayá called me to her to put on my bathing suit. Happily I began to run toward her. Before I arrived at the spot where she was, I was stopped by an arm, by my New Friend; and my whole little being was filled with the most vivid presence of Our Lord, who made me understand that I should not accompany the group. As I stopped, I said to Dona Nayá: "No, Dona Nayá, I do not wish to undress or to go swimming. I shall wait here." At this Dona Nayá naturally was irritated, and she urged me to join the group. I was fearful, timid and undecided as to whether I should obey her or not. I still felt imprisoned by the holy hand of my New Friend. Then I made up my mind and answered decisively: "Dona Nayá, I do not want to undress or to go swimming."

Many members of the group were now ready to enter the water. My New Friend placed himself in front of me. During the whole time that the swimmers remained in the water or on the banks of the river, where they danced, I had for the first time in front of me *the holy and protecting shade* which I supposed was formed by the extended wings of my New Friend. From that day on, these "holy, protecting wings" were always extended in front of me to hinder me from seeing whatever Our Lord or my New Friend did not wish me to see.

At the Movies

In the year 1912 Jaguarão experienced the beginning of the movie rage. On all sides, new movie theaters were being opened. On Sundays there were matinees practically every hour. Intense competition and rivalry sprang up between the various owners. Finally, the firm of Pinto and Brother opened up the most luxurious theater of all. Mr. Pinto was a very rich man. His theater was completely new, with cushioned seats, electric ventilators, waiting rooms and so forth; and all this was for the same price as the others. The name of this theater was Ponto Chic.

Naturally crowds began to throng to the Ponto Chic. On Sundays the matinees were exclusively for the children, to whom the owner distributed beautiful little bags of bonbons. He also raffled off costly prizes, such as a big doll, a pair of skates, etc. This attracted all the children of Jaguarão. I do not know whether this movie fever began to undermine the morals of the people. I only know that on a certain Sunday the priests of the parish announced the opening of another movie theater. The price was to be less than half the price of the other theaters; so this began to draw the people. To this day I remember all of the films that I saw at the Padres' Theater during my childhood and girlhood, including the titles of each one.

Some of the films I saw there were: "The Pub-
lic Life of the Saviour," "The Prodigal Son,"
"The Miracle of the Virgin" and "The Sky for
My Roof."

I cannot say the same of the films that I saw
in the other theaters. With the exception of
films of travel or of natural history, I could not
understand the majority of them, because the
greater part of them was hidden from me by
the "holy wings" of my New Friend. My New
Friend exercised this censorship for the first
time, as we have seen, in Santa Vitória. The second veiling of my eyes took place in the Ponto
Chic Theater. After that it took place all through
my girlhood and young womanhood.

The second occasion came about in this manner: One Sunday the management of the Ponto
Chic Theater announced a very special program. A great number of families came to see
this extra-special program, and we were among
the audience. The title of the film was "Cell
Number 13." The picture began, but only two
or three scenes had flashed on the screen when
at a given moment I felt the holy hand of my
New Friend upon my shoulder. Then, just as at
the waterfall, his "holy wings" were extended in
front of me, hiding completely from my eyes
the scenes that were being projected on the
screen. My New Friend remained thus during
the rest of the film, so that I saw no other scene
of the picture.

On other occasions when I attended the theater his "holy wings" were extended in front of me only for a certain period of time. Then, they were folded, as it were, and I could again see the screen. Yet his holy hand remained on my shoulder, so that I thought more about him than of what was going on around me. For it was he who filled me with happiness, since I knew now that Jesus was satisfied with His little friend. Many times during the showing of a film my New Friend's "holy wings" were extended in front of me for a short time and then taken away, allowing me once more to see what was on the screen.

Not only during the showing of movies did my New Friend act thus but also during plays and other stage exhibitions. How often did my mother call me a simpleton because I could not describe the film or the play which I attended! And my father said to me: "My child, you should be able to describe what you see and to narrate what you hear." Never did I tell them that it was my New Friend who prevented me from seeing what was on the screen or on the stage.

* * *

MY holy and most faithful New Friend, only today do I realize the innumerable dangers to which I was exposed in that evil world and from which I escaped unharmed, solely on account of the special grace of my God and thy most faithful protection. O my God, mayest Thou be eternally glorified in the weakness of Thy little creature! And to thee, my New Friend, I give my grateful love, the love of thy little sister and friend. Amen.

Chapter 12

The Spouse of Jesus

IN THE year 1913 a certain lieutenant colonel arrived in Jaguarão from Rio de Janeiro. He was between forty and fifty years of age, a bachelor and a very rich man. He had been an intimate friend of my father from the time that they were students. He became a frequent visitor at our house. In fact, he came nearly every day to talk with my father in the evening, since our house was only a short distance from the barracks.

Two or three months after his arrival he began to show particular attention to my little person, frequently bringing me costly presents. One day I was called to the parlor by my mother. The lieutenant colonel was there and he wished to give me the present that he had brought me. This was a big box containing a complete trousseau in the latest style, which he had ordered especially from Montevideo. I extended my hand to thank him. He kissed my hand and said to my father: "I like your daughter very much and I wish to make her my wife." I did not understand the meaning of what he said. So with great pleasure I went to show my present to my dear Acácia.

Some days after this I was summoned again to the parlor. The lieutenant colonel was there, dressed in his red and blue uniform. My mother told Acácia to put on me the dress that the lieutenant colonel had brought me. He wished to see if it looked well on me. I must say here quite frankly that I did not like that dress, because it made me look like a young woman. The dress was longer than the ones I was accustomed to wear, and the fine little varnished buttons were of military style, a type I had never used in my life. I had always let my hair fall loose. Acácia curled it every night with great care, but now my mother ordered Acácia to tie it behind with a ribbon.

Thus transformed, I appeared in the parlor. The lieutenant colonel seemed to like me dressed up in this fashion. Opening a little box of blue velvet, he took out a small ring with two diamonds and placed it on my finger, saying: "You are still too young to wear a real engagement ring." At that time I understood neither the meaning of the ring nor the remark. I know only that I was very pleased with the small ring. The lieutenant colonel continued speaking, saying: "Shortly you will travel to Europe. Therefore you must study Italian and German, and learn to play the piano." I was already studying French in school. Some days afterward I began the study of Italian with a special teacher, and the study of the piano with another teacher. A piano was rented for practicing. At school I began to study German under the tutelage of my beloved Mother Raphael.

Some days went by, and one night my father called me. He wished to speak to me alone. He was very serious and apprehensive. He appeared much different from what he usually was. Seating himself, he caressed me tenderly and said to me: "My child, I have important news for you. My friend the lieutenant colonel wishes to make you his wife when you complete fifteen years. I wish you to accept this offer of marriage, which will make you very happy. I know my friend very well, and I am certain that he will make you very happy."

I understood little or nothing of what my father had said. I was only thirteen years old, and up to that time I had never thought about becoming the wife of anyone. In fact, I did not even know what it meant to be a wife. I knew only that my mother was the wife of my father. Therefore, not in the least understanding what my father had said, I answered him as if it were the most trivial of questions, "Yes, Father." Then I left the room without thinking further of the matter.

On the first Friday following the talk with my father, I went, as was my custom, to Holy Mass and received Holy Communion. Soon after receiving Holy Communion, which filled me with joy, I heard these words: "You will not be a wife on this earth, but you will be the spouse of Jesus." I heard and understood these words in the same way that I was accustomed to hear my New Friend speaking to me, but this time it was not he but Our Lord who had spoken.

From that day I thought continually how I could be the spouse of Jesus, for neither did I understand what it meant to be His spouse. A great desire, a burning desire remained in me from that day forward to be the spouse of Jesus. I did realize clearly that if I wanted to be the spouse of Jesus I could not be the wife of the colonel, whose presence was beginning to annoy me. I took a great dislike to wearing the ring after the following incident: On the Sunday after that first Friday, I was getting ready to take a walk with some of my young friends. I took up the ring to put it on my finger, but my New Friend prevented me by gently keeping one hand away from the other. I then put the ring aside with the firm intention of not wearing it any more.

It was not long until the lieutenant colonel noticed that I was not wearing the ring. He told me that he wished me to wear it always. My mother ordered me to put it on and not to take it off any more. I went to get it. Returning to the parlor, I put it on my finger there. My New Friend did not prevent me from putting it on then. But at that moment, in the presence of the lieutenant colonel whom I now found so displeasing, and in the presence of my mother and father, I sought to see the holy face of my New Friend and I perceived that he was displeased with my wearing the ring. I felt a great sadness in my soul. That night as I lay in bed weeping, I asked my new Friend to make me lose the ring.

In a short time the winter arrived, and my hands became covered with chilblains. These swelled up and my ring finger became red. Then my father filed the ring, but he filed it very close to one of the diamonds, so that the beauty of the ring was spoiled. He did not send the ring to be fixed.

I must add here that neither before nor after this incident did I ever have chilblains on my hands. The fingers became so swollen that it was impossible to twist the ring on my finger. Only where the two diamonds were set in the ring, could it be filed without cutting my finger. When the ring was thus filed, its value was destroyed. Encouraged by my success in getting rid of the ring, I now asked my New Friend to free me of the lieutenant colonel.

In a small room near the parlor I had a complete doll's house. One afternoon I was arranging this. I did not notice that the parlor door had opened and that the lieutenant colonel was in the parlor. Seeing me, he came to watch me play. I still did not notice him, as he stood behind me. Then he spoke softly: "You are getting too old for playing with dolls. You are already promised in marriage. You should devote yourself to the study of languages and to practicing the piano. Within two years, we shall travel to Europe." Completely surprised, I turned around to face him. My New Friend drew closer to me. I perceived him. Then, without fearing to displease my father or mother, I answered the lieutenant colonel: "You may as well know that I do not want to be your wife; neither do I wish to study Italian with that professor. I am going to ask my father to stop all this."

These words made the colonel somewhat angry and he answered me: "You do not know what you are saying. You are still too much of a child. Your father will not pay any attention to you." At this I felt my New Friend impelling me gently toward the parlor. Obeying my New Friend, I left the lieutenant colonel alone.

That same day I spoke with my father. Weeping, I threw my arms around his neck and told him that I did not want to be the wife of the lieutenant colonel or to study Italian with the professor. My father embraced me and said to me: "My child, I will not force you to do this; but I want you to understand that if you do not become the wife of the lieutenant colonel you are giving up the opportunity of marrying a gentleman who is very rich, and who can be of great help to your brothers. However, if you do not want this, tomorrow I myself will speak to my friend."

The lieutenant colonel was very unwilling to give up the idea of marrying me. His visits and attempts at persuasion caused me much suffering. Within a short time he was transferred to Rio, and I was left in peace. I rejoiced at his departure and did not forget to thank my New Friend for this favor. But I still did not know how I could become the spouse of Jesus. In time, however, I came to know this.

*   *   *

On December 8, 1914, I became a Child of Mary, receiving the beautiful Miraculous Medal suspended from a wide blue ribbon. I was received into this Sodality by Padre Godofredo Evers, who was still the director. The evening before the reception I had gone to Confession to Padre Godofredo, who said to me afterward: "Tomorrow the good God and His most holy Mother will give you another great and very special grace. But a still greater one is reserved for you. It is the extraordinary grace to become the spouse of Jesus. Do you wish to accept this loving invitation of your God?" I answered: "Padre, for a long time I have wanted to become the spouse of Jesus, and I know already that I shall not be the wife of anyone here on earth."

Then Padre Godofredo explained to me how I could become the spouse of Jesus. I under-

Cecy Cony (Sister Maria Antonia) as a child.

Cecy Cony at the age of twenty.

stood him as far as my limited intelligence allowed me. Padre Godofredo told me to return to the confessional after the last penitent. I did this and he gave me a piece of paper, saying: "Tomorrow, after Holy Communion, repeat to Our Lady the words that I have written on this piece of paper." I learned the prayer by heart, and on the following day I did as he had told me. After Holy Communion, I prayed:

"My most holy Mother, today thou wilt receive me into the number of thy chosen children. I thank thee, beloved Mother, and I wish to make a bargain. Today, when I shall kneel at the foot of thy altar, when the servant and minister of thy Son shall give me, in thy name, thy Miraculous Medal and the title of Child of Mary, I shall entrust to thy most pure hands the lily of my innocence and virginity. Guard my virginity, O most holy Mary, for it is thine. I shall never take it back. And when my Divine Spouse shall come to claim it from me, then, O Virgin of virgins, I shall answer my Spouse happily: 'I have confided it to Thy virginal Mother. She will give it to Thee.'"

During the ceremony of reception, when, as I was kneeling at the foot of the altar, Padre Godofredo offered me the medal to kiss, I repeated with my heart the above prayer. During the whole ceremony my New Friend rested his holy hand on my shoulder. Our Lord was with me as in Holy Communion; Our Lady was also with me, although I did not see them.

On the same day Padre Godofredo asked me after the celebration if I had entrusted my virginity to Our Lady. In a low voice I answered him: "The holy Angel rested his holy hand on my shoulder, while with the other he handed a lily to Our Lady." I saw tears in Padre Godofredo's eyes, but he wiped them away quickly. I do not know, however, why those tears came.

Chapter 13

The Annual School Picnic

IN THE year 1913 we were preparing for our annual school picnic on October 25 in honor of the feast day of Mother Raphael. This annual excursion into the country was enjoyed by all the students. Each student was fortified with the indispensable small basket of sandwiches. In that year of 1913 I was not accompanied by my sisters. Dilsa had died four years before, in 1909, and Gizelda had graduated from the school. Acácia prepared my basket with a variety of good things to eat, especially with those that she knew I liked. At the appointed hour of mid-day I set out joyfully for the school.

I was walking alone. In one hand I carried the basket; in the other I held a canvas bag filled with apples and bananas. I was passing by a corner a short distance from the school when I saw seated on the pavement an old woman, begging. Stretching out her hand, she said to me: "Little girl, give an alms to a poor old woman who has not had a cup of coffee yet today." I happened to have in my apron pocket the change left over from buying fruit. My mother had allowed me to keep this change, which was not very much. I gave it to the old woman, who received it gratefully, saying: "May our Lord bless you!"

I continued on my way happily, but I had not gone ten steps when I stopped in surprise. My New Friend had gently placed his holy hand on my shoulder. I understood that he wished something. I sought his holy face, and it was sad but not severe. At the same instant I thought of the old woman sitting at the corner. I looked back and she was still there. Then I thought: "How can that poor woman obtain enough food for today and tomorrow with the little money I gave her? I should give her everything that I have brought with me for the picnic. Only in this way can I take away the sadness from the holy face of my New Friend."

I returned to the beggar, and with unaccustomed haste I emptied into her lap everything that I had in the basket and in the bag, while I said to her: "I had brought all this food for our picnic, but I want to give it all to you, since you did not have breakfast yet." I do not know what the poor old woman answered; I noticed only her gesture of great surprise. Then I began to run toward the school, as if I feared I should not have the necessary will power to do faithfully what my New Friend desired. Arriving at the corner of the school, I stopped, and once again I sought the holy face of my New Friend. It was not sad any more; it possessed that "sweetness" which told me that Our Lord and my New Friend were happy with their little friend. I opened the basket and put the empty canvas bag into it. Then I thought: "How can I go to the school and on the picnic with an empty basket?"

I made up my mind to return home and ask Acácia to fill my basket a second time. I knew that she would do this for me. I was about to run home when again I felt the most sweet hand of my New Friend hindering me. He did not wish me to return but to continue on to the school. I obeyed him, although my mind was confused and undecided, thinking of what I should say to the other students when they saw my empty basket. I knew that they would make fun of me. This was the great fear which vexed my soul, but the sweet expression on the holy face of my New Friend drove my fears away. I entered the school as happy as if my basket were still full of the good things I liked so well.

The schoolyard was already filled with children, and each one was carrying a small basket. Then I wished I had at least a piece of bread to hold down the bottom of the basket; for it was so light that it was difficult to carry it without someone's noticing that it was empty. The baskets of the other children were so filled that they could scarcely be closed. I spent some fearful moments wondering what I should do at the picnic spot when the children divided up into groups to eat their lunch.

Shortly, we set out on our picnic. I was with my group of seven or eight children. During the walk each one told the others what she had brought for her lunch, while I remained silent and embarrassed. We finally arrived at the spot for the picnic. Then it was soon time for lunch. All the children spread out in groups over the grass. I stood still, undecided whether or not I should join my group. I sought the holy face of my New Friend, seeking help and guidance from him. The holy "sweetness" which filled my soul with such great joy put my indecision to flight. (I realize now what I did not recognize then, namely, that my fear came from my dislike of being humiliated by my companions.)

I went toward the members of my group, who were calling me. My New Friend wished this. All of them had their baskets opened and were already eating. One of them took hold of my basket to see what it contained. What was her surprise and my annoyance! Everyone saw that the basket was empty, containing only the empty canvas bag. All began to laugh loudly, while I could hardly keep back the tears and sobs. I wanted to ask them not to laugh at me. A thousand questions came at me from all sides, accompanied by stinging remarks:

"Did you hide your lunch in a hole in the ground in case we should ask you for something?"

"She ate her own lunch and now she wants to share ours."

"I thought there was something peculiar about the way she swung the basket back in the school-yard."

"Did you have no food at home to bring on the picnic?"

I could not stand any more. I would tell everything to Mother Raphael. The girls were very unkind to me. But the holy hand of my New Friend prevented me from leaving and speaking to Mother Raphael. How I wished that I could at least leave this group and join another! My New Friend did not want me to do that; so I remained with my own group.

Overcoming my will with a tremendous effort, I seated myself once again. One of the girls offered me a big piece of jellied fruit on a slice of cheese. Immediately the thought arose in my mind: "I will not accept it; I do not need her food." But before I had time to say one word, I felt resting on my shoulder that holy hand so well known to me. I understood that my New Friend wished me to accept the offered food. Within me there was a battle between my will and my self-love. My will conquered. I accepted what was offered to me. I accepted also what the other girls offered me. Whenever I took a mouthful of food, I did not taste the sweetness of those good things because of the violent repugnance I felt within me. However, the "sweet-

ness" of the holy face of my New Friend over-
came everything. The picnic came to an end,
and no one knew what had happened; neither
my father, nor my mother, nor Mother Raphael,
nor Acácia, nor anyone at all.

Chapter 14

Sacrifices for Our Lady

AT THE beginning of the school year in 1914 Padre Godofredo said to me in my first Confession after the opening of school: "You must begin at once to prepare yourself to receive the great grace of making your profession as a Child of Mary next December." I had been received as an aspirant in the Sodality of the Children of Mary in December, 1913. Continuing, he said: "Do not allow one little sacrifice to pass by without offering it to Our Lady." On the afternoon of that very day our heavenly Mother asked the first small sacrifice of her little child.

My New School Kit

On arriving home from school, I found upon my desk a package which my father had bought for me. It was a beautiful student's supply kit, made of varnished wood and containing pencils, a ruler, pen, penknife, erasers, paper, a pen cleaner, extra pen nibs, a supply of pencil leads—in fine, everything that a student would need. Since the previous year I had wished to have such a kit. I had seen several, as some of the other students already owned them. More than once I had told my father what I wanted.

How great was my happiness when I finally owned such a student's kit! I spent hours admiring my new treasure. Before the usual time I began to prepare my lessons solely for the pleasure of using my marvelous supply case. My old case now seemed ugly and useless. I did not want to use it any more. I resolved to give it, with everything in it, to Padre Domingos after Mass on the following day. He would be glad to get it for the poor students of his night school.

I had finished my lessons for the following day. Still overflowing with happiness, I began to clean and arrange the old case. Then I wrapped it up neatly, so that it was ready to be taken to Padre Domingos. When it was wrapped up in the very same paper that I had taken off the new case, and tied with the very same twine, I placed it on my desk. Then I was suddenly assaulted by a heart-rending thought: "Instead of giving the old case to Padre Domingos, why should I not give him the new one?" This daring and sickening idea was immediately succeeded by another thought, which tried to stifle the first one: "No! I cannot do that. Padre Domingos always asks for schoolbooks and school supplies for which we have no further use."

Now my mind began to wage a bitter battle. I was completely opposed to the first idea. I thought of another objection to it: "I need this new student's supply case, as I am now in a higher class and nearly all the students have similar school sets." My mind was made up. I would take the old case to Padre Domingos. I picked it up to take it to my room, as if I wanted to add assurance to my decision.

I had not reached the threshold of the door when the holy hand of my New Friend descended gently on my shoulder and a new thought entered my mind: "This could be the first small sacrifice made in honor of my heavenly Mother, that I might deserve to be professed as a Child of Mary." My mind ceased to be troubled by conflicting thoughts. I looked at the holy face of my New Friend, which presented that aspect of severity customary when my Guardian Angel was awaiting some generous decision from his little friend. I understood and made my decision accordingly. I resolved to take the new school supply kit to Padre Domingos. He could use it as a prize for the best student in his night school. I returned to my desk and seated myself. In a few moments I had wrapped and tied the new school set just as I had received it. Before I took it to my room, I looked at the holy face of my New Friend. The "sweetness" I saw thereon repaid me a hundredfold for my small sacrifice. On the following day at the end of Holy Mass I did not return to school with the other children, as I had to speak to Padre Domingos. He seemed to have expected my small gift, for he gave me a beautiful holy picture of the Blessed Virgin. This made me very happy, for Our Lady seemed to say that she had accepted with great joy the small sacrifice I had offered to her.

A Pair of Skates

The following incident took place in the year 1914. With the approach of winter the owners of the Salão Ponto Chic opened a skating rink. Alice, one of my friends, invited me to attend the celebration which marked its inauguration. We went, and I was enchanted by the sight of the great crowd of boys and girls, girls even of my own age, who were gliding swiftly and gracefully around the big rink of polished mosaic. Ah, how I wished I could skate also! It should be great fun. At that moment, while I was admiring the skillfulness of the skaters, I resolved not to spend a penny until I had saved the twenty-five cruzeiros necessary to buy a pair of skates. From then on the skating rink began to attract me, just as formerly I had been drawn to the main square for rides in my little automobile. Every Sunday, at five o'clock in the afternoon, I was to be found at the skating rink in the company of Alice. One Sunday when Alice came to call for me, she was the proud owner of a beautiful new shining pair of skates, which she had just bought the day before.

Finally I had saved enough money to buy a pair of skates. My desire to own a pair was so great that on that joyful day I judged that there was no one more happy in the world than I was. To buy them I had to wait until Saturday, when there was no school in the afternoon. Then I could go into the shopping district with Alice and buy them in the very same shop where she had bought hers. On Sunday I would try out the new skates during the period reserved for beginners.

The following Saturday was clear and brisk. At two o'clock in the afternoon Alice and I were seated in the rowboat which would ferry us across to the shopping district. I was looking forward to a quick return with the skates. Before the boat was shoved off, a new passenger took his seat in the boat. He was well known to me. That morning he had forgiven all the sins I had committed during the previous week. I greeted Padre Godofredo. I wished to arise, but the rocking of the boat prevented me. He returned my greeting and added, "Cecy, what are you doing here?" In my great joy, I answered: "Padre, I am going to buy a pair of skates." The boat was pushed off and Padre Godofredo began to read or to say his breviary. We crossed over the River Jaguarão. When we stepped ashore,

Padre Godofredo drew me aside and said: "Our Lady expects a sacrifice."

These words, so unexpected, caused more consternation than if a bomb had been dropped at my feet. I stood on the dock without being able to take one step forward as another battle began to be waged within me. Alice became impatient. All I could say to her, was, "Wait a little while!" My mind was in a whirl, filled with conflicting thoughts, just as in the case of the new student's supply kit, which I liked so much.

Oh, no! Our Lady could not ask me to give up buying the pair of skates I desired so much. I had already offered her the new student's supply kit. How could I give up buying the skates, upon which I had set my heart? I would make another sacrifice instead of this one.

I made my decision. "Let's go quickly!" I said to Alice. Before we reached the shop, I remembered to look at the holy face of my New Friend. It had that look of compassionate severity which made me understand what my Guardian Angel expected of his little friend. Sorrow filled my heart and a new thought surged through my mind: "O Mother of Heaven, I ask pardon from thee. Dost thou not then deserve this sacrifice of the skates? I was thinking it was too much to offer thee." I felt the most sincere sorrow in my soul and I could hardly keep back the tears.

Alice, tired of waiting, gave me a push and said: "Cecy, my patience is at an end. Are you coming or are you going to stay here all day? You seem to have fallen asleep."

"Alice," I answered, "let us return home. I do not want to buy the skates now. I have resolved to do something else."

Alice was startled. "Are you crazy?" she asked. "We came all this way to buy them; so let's buy them."

"No, Alice, I do not want to buy them now. I will buy you a jar of caramels, and then we shall return home."

This made Alice agreeable to the change in plans. We entered a candy shop and bought the caramels. Then we returned home. I now had twenty cruzeiros. I knew what I should do in order to make amends for my unwillingness to sacrifice the skates. When Alice left me at the corner of her house, I went to a nearby store and changed my money into small coins. Then I went to the asylum that sheltered the poor who had no homes, and I distributed the coins to each poor person in that part of the build-ing where my friend Cyprian Joseph had died. Each poor person was very happy to receive my small offering, but my own happiness was incom-parably greater. I am convinced that the plea-sure which I would have received from the new pair of skates would have been much less than the "sweetness" I received from my New Friend.

Incidents such as the above happened many times. To narrate each one seems unnecessary.

Chapter 15

The Beggarwoman

IN THE year 1915 there lived in Jaguarão a beggarwoman who was about fifty years old. She was noted for her repulsive physical ugliness. The children looked upon her as a witch or a sorceress from the storybooks. They feared her greatly. Because of her extreme talkativeness they called her "Bate-bico" [which could be translated as "Beak-beater"].

Oftentimes during the long evenings of summer, when I was studying in the garden, I would hear the boys shouting: "Bate-bico. Look at Bate-bico!" Then the poor woman would become furious, throwing stones at them and vowing vengeance on them. I would stop studying for a while, filled with sadness and sympathy for the miserable life of that poor woman. I would begin to think: "Perhaps when she was a little girl, she did not have any home or any parents to take care of her. Or after her parents died, she became this way." Then I would be filled with the fear of losing my parents or of being separated from them.

Mother Raphael had told us many times that an ugly exterior could hide a most beautiful soul. "Perhaps this poor woman has a soul as white as mine was on the day of my First Holy Communion," I would think, "and her Guardian Angel is always pleased with her, and Our Lord is going to take her to Heaven. But because she is ugly and dirty, the boys on the street think that her soul is in the same condition." These thoughts returned each time I heard the boys shouting "Bate-bico." Every week this beggarwoman went to the carpentry shop, from which she returned carrying on her shoulders a big sack filled with pieces of wood. These she used to cook her meals.

One afternoon Alice and I took a walk down to the skating rink. We did not have any skates, so we were just watching the skaters. Suddenly I heard whistling and laughter from the street. I ran to the big iron gate, which was open. Looking out, I saw the poor beggarwoman carrying the big sack of pieces of wood. Tied to the sack was a long piece of cloth knotted around an old tin can. When the beggarwoman walked along, she dragged behind her the tin can which made plenty of noise. In a few seconds the gate and the footpath were filled with boys and girls laughing at the ridiculous state of the poor woman.

As for me I felt more like weeping than laughing, but I kept the tears back, because I was afraid that those present would make fun of me for weeping when everyone was laughing. The poor woman continued to walk, although the weight of the sack was bowing her down and she was in danger of being tripped by that long piece of cloth dragging the tin can over the stones of the street. Seeing this, I thought: "If I could only tear that piece of cloth from the sack!" I put this thought from me with great displeasure, saying to myself: "No! I could not do that. Everyone would see me, and that group of boys would yell at me. How embarrassed I should be! What a sight I would be—running down the street after the beggarwoman, pushing my way through those boys. I could not even think of doing that."

Then I felt resting on my head the holy hand of my New Friend, and as if he whispered to me, I heard the words: "If you were in the place of that poor woman, how you would like to be freed from that ridiculous and humiliating state by some charitable hand! Go; Jesus asks this from you!"

I looked toward the poor woman and measured the distance which separated me from her. It was the distance of one street to another. The crowd of boys seemed to me to have increased. I saw people at all the doors and windows. I looked at my New Friend. His holy face held that look of severity combined with sadness. He was expecting something of me. I saw nothing more. Without wishing to do it, I said to Alice: "I am going to untie that piece

The parish church at Jaguarão.

Padre Godofredo Evers
of the Order of Premonstratensians,
spiritual director of Cecy Cony
during her school days.

of cloth from the sack of the beggarwoman."

Pulling me by the dress, Alice said: "Are you crazy? They will yell at you just like they are yelling at Bate-bico."

I saw nothing more. I heard nothing else. I began to run after the poor woman, who was walking along, followed by her tormentors. Without thinking what would be the best way to untie the cloth, I reached the tin can first of all. Taking it in my hand, I tried to tear the cloth. The beggarwoman felt the pull; and thinking, perhaps, that the boys were trying to pull the sack from her shoulders, she gave a strong pull to the sack in her direction. The result was that the edge of the can dug into my arm and gave me a deep cut. I still have the scar today.

At this I ran up to the poor woman and tried to explain what I was doing, but she did not understand and became very angry. I became speechless with shame. I heard the yelling of the boys and I felt as if hundreds of eyes were watching me as one of the principal actresses in this contemptible scene. Finally it seemed that the beggarwoman understood that I wanted to help her. I wished to return to the rink, but the holy hand of my New Friend would not permit me. My Guardian Angel wished me to untie the piece of cloth from the sack. The poor woman, who was no longer angry at me, now permitted me to untie the cloth. Moved by this act of kindness, she said: "Many thanks, little girl. There is still someone in this world who has pity on me." Then I forgot my shame. I helped her put the sack on her shoulders and I returned to the rink.

Only then did I notice the blood running down my arm and staining my dress. Alice tied my handkerchief around the cut. Fearing that she might tell my mother everything, I returned home alone. Arriving there, I was able to enter unnoticed by the garden gate. I put arnica in water and bathed the cut, which was paining me. While I was doing this, my New Friend rested his holy hand on my head. I looked at his holy face, and as I perceived the "sweetness' thereon, I heard, as it were, this phrase being whispered: "Jesus is satisfied with His little friend." This filled me with happiness and I thought no more of the pain in my arm.

In my next Confession I told everything to Padre Godofredo. At the end of my narration he said to me: "Let us make a contract which will be signed by Jesus. Tomorrow, Sunday, you will take care of the body of that poor woman, attending to her cleanliness and dress, and I will take care of her soul."

What luck, I thought, that I still had ten cruzeiros which my father had given me. With this money I could buy sandals, stockings, garters and soap. I could get a dress and other clothing from my mother. On the following day, after Holy Mass, everything was ready. I did not forget a scissors and some brilliantine, as the woman's hair seemed never to have been combed. I took also some bread and some marmalade. I set out for the asylum. Arriving there, I found poor Bate-bico squatting at the door of her room. What a sight! She was horribly dirty. When I entered the room with her to show her what I had brought, my stomach began to roll with nausea and I had to use every effort to keep from vomiting.

"Dona Maria," I said, "I want to make you very pretty and clean. I brought you some scented soap and brilliantine." The poor woman became radiant with happiness. However, I was going to find my part of the contract extremely difficult. I did not know where to begin at my job of cleaning her. I asked her for a basin and she brought me a very small one. I gave her the soap and told her to wash her face first. She was not opposed to this and seemed to like the scent of the soap, but she did not wash her face thoroughly.

Then I had a good idea. My handkerchief was still clean and folded. I fetched clean water and rubbed soap on the handkerchief. Then I myself cleaned the neck and the ears of the poor woman with the soapy handkerchief. At the end of my rubbing, I told her to wash away the soap with water. I wished to do the same with her feet. I seated her and gave her the soapy handkerchief to wash her feet, because my stomach was pitching and rolling with nausea. I felt sick and dizzy. I went outside, thinking: "I cannot stand this nausea. I shall tell Padre Godofredo the job is too difficult for me." I was going to leave, when the holy hand of my New Friend led me gently by the shoulder back into the room. I thought immediately: "The contract was signed by Jesus. I must fulfill it in so far as I can."

Returning to the room, I found the beggar-woman diligently washing her feet with the soapy handkerchief, which was now completely black. The water was also horribly filthy; so I brought some clean water. In the deformed feet there were many cuts. The toenails were excessively long and encrusted with dirt. Dona Maria dried her feet with an old rag that was not clean. Now I had to cut the nails on her fingers and toes. I took out the scissors. I wanted to begin with her fingernails. I began, but the retchings of my stomach could be restrained no longer. Without having time to leave the room, my stomach relieved itself, soiling my dress. The holy hand of my New Friend rested on my head.

With a superhuman effort I cut the finger-nails and toenails. There remained only the job of arranging the woman's hair. When I looked at that wretched disheveled head, I nearly lost courage. However, the holy hand of my New Friend continued resting gently upon my head, soothing and strengthening me. I dipped my fingers in the brilliantine, but when I turned to rub it into the hair, that hair which was so dirty and smelly, I again became sick. My hands, which were greasy with the brilliantine, filled me with disgust. I cannot describe the sensation I felt while I arranged the hair of that poor woman. I cannot describe what I saw on that poor wretched head, which seemed more like that of some unclean animal than of a human being.

Finally, it was finished. Now Dona Maria could put on the clean clothes. I told her to change her clothing while I went outside to wash my greasy hands, which I found so nauseating. When I returned, I told her to put on the stockings and the sandals. My mother's dress fitted her fairly well, except that it was a little big for her. Then I said to her: "Now you are clean and beautiful; so you can eat the bread and marmalade." She was as meek as a lamb, and everything caused her to smile and laugh.

Having finished my part of the contract, I ran home. I was ashamed of the state in which I was. It was now my turn to appear dirty and disheveled. During that whole day my New Friend did not take his holy hand from my head. It seemed as if I were in Heaven. Our Lord remained with me as in Holy Communion.

That same Sunday afternoon Padre Godofredo visited the beggarwoman. On the following Saturday, during my Confession, he said to me:

"The good Jesus is not sorry for having signed our contract. He is most pleased with His little friend. The soul of that poor woman is now shining. She received Holy Communion on Monday. I do not think that she will live much longer; so I shall visit her often. But you must not go there any more."

On the next day, which was Sunday, when I arrived home after hearing Holy Mass, I was surprised with the news that Dona Maria had been stricken with an attack when she was returning from the church. They carried her to the asylum, but she was dead when she arrived there. I wept secretly out of pity for that poor woman and perhaps also from sorrow at losing her. Every time I prayed for her soul, my New Friend rested his holy hand gently on my head. This happened for a long time, until finally he ceased to do this. Then I thought: "Dona Maria has now gone to Heaven."

May Our Lord be glorified in the faithfulness of my New Friend and in the weakness of His little creature, who did nothing through herself!

Chapter 16

Another Sacrifice for Our Lady

A T THE end of that chapter in which I told about the sacrifice of the skates, I added a note that there had been many incidents such as this. Hence, I thought it unnecessary to narrate all of them. But, since I have been told to narrate everything, I shall do so.

Let us return, therefore, to the year 1914, the year of sacrifices for Our Lady. Every month when he received his pay, my father was accustomed to give each one of us five cruzeiros, with which we could buy whatever we wanted. It gave me great pleasure to use "my own money," as I considered it, for my personal purchases. Only rarely did I ask my father or mother for the things I desired, as I preferred to wait until I had saved up enough money to buy whatever I wanted.

I do not know whether this was a good or a bad inclination. I only know that I received greater pleasure from using "my own money" to buy what I desired than from having my father buy it. My mother said this was a special mania of mine, but my father affirmed that it demonstrated a certain spirit of independence, and he was not opposed to my acting thus. Whichever it was, I continued with my mania, if you agreed with my mother; or with my spirit of independence, if you seconded my father. What is more to the point is that my New Friend busied himself several times with this trait of mine. But, to continue my story:

The monthly payday was a time of great excitement for us, and I always had something in mind that I wanted to buy with "my fortune." One afternoon I went to a furniture store to buy a plaything called *o diávolo*, which all the children were buying at that time. I told the man what I wanted: one just like Alice's, with the two pieces of stick covered with metal at the end where the cord was tied, and the edges of the bobbin covered with rubber to keep it from being broken when it fell. I was very happy with my purchase and I thought: "I will take my *diávolo* to Alice's house and we shall play a game." I had ten cruzeiros when I entered the store. I paid seven cruzeiros for the *diávolo*; so there were three cruzeiros left to buy chocolate. We played for bars of chocolate.

A Broken Bottle of Kerosene

I set out for Alice's house. I had covered about half the distance when I met a poor girl about my own age. She was dirty and ragged and was weeping over the broken pieces of a bottle of kerosene, which lay spilled upon the ground. Out of sympathy I stopped before this sad scene, now looking at the weeping girl, now looking at the broken pieces of bottle. It was she who broke the silence, saying: "I went to buy a bottle of kerosene for a neighbor who promised me a few pennies. Now I don't have any money to buy more kerosene, and I won't get the money promised to me, and my mother will beat me."

I felt a great pity for the poor girl, and I remembered joyfully that I still had the three cruzeiros with which I was going to buy the chocolate. As if it were a ten-cruzeiro note, I said to the girl: "Wait here for me. I shall run over to the drug store to change my money. Then I shall give you money to buy more kerosene; so don't cry any more." The girl quickly dried her tears on the edge of her dress, and in a few seconds she was smiling and showing her snow-white teeth.

I came back with a fistful of change. I asked the girl the price of the bottle of kerosene, and she answered: "Sixty centavos, but the bottle belonged to our neighbor. It would cost another twenty centavos." I replied: "I shall give you half of my change. Give eighty centavos to your neighbor, and you can keep the other seventy centavos." But at the very moment that I placed the cruzeiro and a half in the hand of the girl,

I felt the holy hand of my New Friend upon my shoulder.

"Wait a minute," I said to the girl, as I perceived that my New Friend wanted me to do something. The girl, surprised and fearful of my indecision, looked at me out of her big, wide eyes. Then the thought came to me: "I should give all my change to this poor girl and that will make her much happier. I will deprive myself of the chocolate as another sacrifice for Our Lady."

"Very well," I said, turning to the girl, "I will give you the whole three cruzeiros." Her face widened in a big smile and her eyes danced with joy. I looked at my New Friend, but I did not receive the "sweetness" that I expected. What, then, did my New Friend want of me? I did not know what else I should do. A few moments passed by, and then I heard in my mind, as it were, these words: "Not only the change, but also the treasured *diávolo*; you should give everything to this poor girl."

Now another struggle began in my mind, as I thought: "How many times already have I given up things that I desired so much! But if I allow this sacrifice in honor of Our Lady to pass by, perhaps I shall not receive the medal and blue ribbon of the Children of Mary." As if a ray of grace had entered my soul, I felt a great repentance for my selfishness, and now, before the wondering girl, I began to weep.

Wishing to hide the motive of my tears, I said to her: "I want to give you all the money that I have with me, and also the money that my father gives me each month." I showed the girl where I lived and asked her to come on the fourth day of each month to receive the five cruzeiros that I would keep for her.

During the whole of that year (1914), until December, I gave this poor girl my precious allowance. In return I received something incomparably more precious, the "sweetness" of my New Friend. During that year I allowed no opportunity for a sacrifice in honor of Our Lady to pass by; and in December Our Lady allowed me to receive the medal and blue ribbon of her children. During the school vacation from December, 1914, to March, 1915, this poor girl said good-by to me, as her family moved to the town of Pelotas.

Chapter 17

The Feast of the Most Holy Spirit

I CANNOT remember exactly in what year the following incident took place. I only know that it happened before the year 1911.

I had a great admiration for a certain colonel who was a friend of my father. Many times I heard my father praising his brave and upright character, his impartial justice toward his subordinates. Every year, at the approach of the Feast of the Most Holy Spirit, the heavenly patron of Jaguarão, the people were accustomed to walk with the banner of the Holy Spirit through the streets, taking up a collection to cover the expenses of the celebration. There was no house, whether rich or poor, no establishment, whether public or private, where they did not enter with this banner to receive the offerings of the faithful and leave there the blessing of the Most Holy Spirit.

In our house it was always I who welcomed the people bearing this sacred banner. When I had placed my father's donation on the tray, I dropped also my own little offering, because I wanted to make a personal gift myself. At the end of the visit I always kissed the banner containing a painting of a beautiful white dove. For three days this banner was carried through the city and the neighborhood.

It was customary also to carry the banner into the barracks, which were situated facing a great square covered with grass, called Barracks' Square. The small procession bearing the banner had already entered this square and was approaching the barracks when the colonel sent a sergeant to tell the group that they should turn back, that the banner would not be received in the barracks. News of this occurrence spread far and wide within a short time. In my house I heard my family talking about it and commenting on it, and for the first time, I heard my father condemn an action of his friend.

As for me, this occurrence left a very strong impression on me, and I could not understand how that colonel could be so bad. In my imagination I saw constantly that sorrowful scene, the banner of the Most Holy Spirit being prohibited from entering the barracks. So great was my sorrow and regret over this insult to the Most Holy Spirit that I was always thinking how I could make the Holy Spirit look with joy and gladness again on Jaguarão. I felt a great pity also for the soldiers who had been deprived of the opportunity to give an offering in honor of the Holy Spirit and to receive His special blessing in return.

I passed the days in sorrowing for the Holy Spirit, and more than once, at night, when I was in bed, I wept bitterly out of pity for the Holy Spirit, who had been banned from the barracks. The feast was approaching and my anxiety increased, because I could not think of some way in which I could bring joy to the Holy Spirit on His feast day. The feast was now only one week away, and yet I did not have any idea of what I should do. I prayed and prayed for light, but my mind could think of nothing.

One night, when I was already in bed and the light had been extinguished, I felt anew in my soul a great pity for the Holy Spirit, who had been cast out, as it were. I sat up in bed and began to weep so much that I could scarcely keep from sobbing. I felt a great and deep sorrow, although I was still only a child. I believe that if at that moment it had been said to me: "You will give joy to the Holy Spirit on His feast day only if you wish to die in a most cruel manner," I would not have refused. My desire to do something to make the Holy Spirit happy was so strong that I was even willing thus to make reparation for the insult given to Him. When I was thus weeping without consolation, the holy hand of my New Friend (who up to that time had not expressed himself), rested with heavenly sweetness upon my head, as if to promise me help.

My tears stopped at once, and that "sweetness" filled my soul, so that I forgot I was still on earth and believed I was already in Heaven. In a short while I fell asleep. On the following day I still had the strong desire to do something to bring gladness to the Holy Spirit. The consolation I had received from my New Friend did not take away my pity for the Holy Spirit. However, I never imagined what my New Friend was going to ask of his little friend that day, which was only three days before the feast.

Early in the morning, when I was taking breakfast, the holy hand of my New Friend rested gently upon my head. At the same instant, I heard, as it were, the whisper of a voice saying: "Those poor soldiers with their simple faith were deprived of the pleasure of giving their offerings and of receiving, with the holy visit, the blessing of the Most Holy Spirit." As oftentimes happened to me, this was a thought, but a thought very different from those that I usually had. It was a thought that seemed to me more like a voice, although it was only a thought.

Then the idea came to me that I should ask each soldier whom I met for an offering for the Feast. In return I should offer to them, to kiss, the medal of the Holy Spirit that I had received during last year's celebration. This was succeeded by another thought: "How embarrassed I should be! What would I look like, stopping the soldiers in the street and asking them for money?" As if in answer, came a third thought: "Even though it cost me much embarrassment, I should do this in order to bring joy to the Holy Spirit on His feast day. I must begin today. Otherwise there will not be enough time to collect the money and take it to the pastor before the feast day."

That afternoon, after taking coffee, I asked my mother for permission to go shopping for the white shoes that my father intended to buy me for this feast. In this way I would be able to meet many soldiers. My mother granted permission. I went toward the shops and took up my stand at the corner of a street. Then I saw a soldier coming toward me. My heart began to pound with embarrassment. I even wished that the soldier would disappear. I was filled with shame, but the holy hand of my New Friend rested gently on my shoulder. This filled me with joy and I forgot everything else. This solder was now only three steps from me—this soldier whom the Holy Spirit had led to me.

"Mister soldier, excuse me!" I said. The politeness of this good soldier encouraged me, and I continued the short talk I had prepared and studied beforehand, which went like this: "I felt great sorrow because the colonel did not allow the banner of the Holy Spirit to enter the barracks." Here I noticed a look of amazement on the soldier's face, but I continued: "And the poor soldiers could neither give their offerings nor salute the banner. I am going to ask all the soldiers whom I meet, to make a small offering. I shall take everything that I receive to the pastor before the feast day."

The good soldier immediately unbuttoned his tunic, and taking out some money, said: "With great pleasure, little girl. Here is my offering." He gave me not just a small coin, but a whole cruzeiro. This made me very happy, and in my happiness I gave my medal to this generous soldier. Only afterward did I remember that now I would not have a medal to offer to the other soldiers to kiss.

My collection that afternoon amounted to the sum of thirty cruzeiros and some centavos, which to me seemed an immense sum of money. None of the good soldiers whom I approached gave me a small coin, which was all I asked, but each one gave me at least a cruzeiro, and some gave two-cruzeiro notes. When I returned home, I guarded my collection in the drawer of my desk. It was made up mostly of coins, which I wished to exchange for a new paper note. This I could place in an envelope and send to the pastor for the feast of the Holy Spirit. I decided that two days before the feast I would go to the office of Mr. Cerqueira and ask him to give me cruzeiro notes for the coins. I wanted one note only, but there was no thirty-cruzeiro note. From twenty-cruzeiro notes there was a jump to fifty-cruzeiro notes. How wonderful it would be if I could get a fifty-cruzeiro note!

Then I had an idea: "Supposing I did not buy those white shoes for the feast day but wore my best pair of black shoes. Then I would have fifty cruzeiros by adding to my collection the twenty cruzeiros my father had given me to buy the white shoes." But, alas! I would not look pretty with a white dress, white stockings, everything white except the black shoes. The Holy Spirit would be happy with what the soldiers themselves had given. I resolved, therefore, that I would buy the white shoes and stockings.

On opening the drawer to take out the collection money and put it into a little paper bag, I felt the holy hand of my New Friend resting on my shoulder. His holy face expected something of me. Yes, I must give up the beautiful white shoes. My father had already given me the twenty cruzeiros. I went to him and told him that I did not wish to buy the white shoes. Then I asked him if I could have the money for myself, and he allowed me to keep it.

I went to the office of Mr. Cerqueira and asked for a new fifty-cruzeiro note. The money that remained over, I placed in the box at the door of the parish church. Returning home, I placed the note in an envelope, which I sealed and upon which I wrote: "Offering of a group of soldiers for the feast of the Most Holy Spirit." Then I took it to the parish church. Since I did not see either the pastor or the sacristan, I left the envelope upon the table in the sacristy.

On the eve of the feast day I had the great joy of reading in the list of offerings: "A group of soldiers—fifty cruzeiros." No one ever discovered my part in this offering. Wearing my black shoes, I took part in the feast. The reward that I received was the most sweet visit of Our Lord, who showed that He was very pleased with His little friend and that He liked me better with the black shoes than if I had worn the prettier white ones. I enjoyed the holy "sweetness" of my New Friend until the octave day of that great feast.

Chapter 18

The Black Domino

DURING the carnival of 1915 the only topics of conversation were the masquerade balls, the parades and the queens of the two clubs, both of whom were friends of mine. When I went walking with my friends, they spoke to me only about their enchanting, fancy dress costumes. Even today I still remember the particular costume that each one was going to wear: Leontina was going as an Egyptian princess; Cléia, as a native of Champagne; Prendinha, as a girl from Alsace; Gizelda, as a Norwegian; one of my aunts, as a student. Prendinha told me about the other groups, the Apaches, the Columbines, the black Dominoes, the Pierrots.

I also became filled with enthusiasm for the carnival. It was my initiation into these social affairs. I told my mother that I wished to dress in a costume like the other girls, and she consented. My aunt was given the task of arranging my costume, which was to be that of a young girl Apache. She gave me the necessary information and some notions of etiquette, saying: "With your group you must take part in the polonaise, for you are now a young woman."

This news filled me with dread, for I could dance only those steps that Acácia had taught us on our big veranda while she hummed and played for all the children of the neighborhood. Looking at my aunt, I tried to explain: "I do not know the polonaise and everyone will laugh at me."

"What of it?" she answered. "That is the best way to learn, and it is time that you began to go to dances."

My enthusiasm began to cool and I think I would have withdrawn from the whole affair if they had not begun to make my costume. In a short time my enthusiasm returned, especially when I saw my friends' fancy dress costumes and my own, which had a skirt of bright red satin, a small apron and blouse of white organdy, and a bodice of black velvet, braided in front with gilded lace. There was a large red silken handkerchief for my head. The stockings were white, and the shoes were a cherry red. When I saw the complete costume laid out, I was in rapture.

At last the great day of the carnival arrived. A bitter rivalry broke out between the two clubs, the Harmonia and the Jaguarense. Each one wanted to outdo the other. This made my mother fearful and she did not want us to take part in the carnival. Finally, the car in which we were to ride, came; and the young men of the committee guaranteed that there would be no trou-

ble. The meeting place was the home of the
queen, outside of which there was an endless
line of decorated cars and a colorful crowd of
people in fancy dress—young men and women,
boys, girls and little children. The members of
the organizing committee were rushing hither
and thither, trying to assign the cars to the different groups.

Two men finally noticed me and led me to
a car in which were seated two girls whom I
did not know. They were dressed in Chinese
costumes. I took my place between the two of
them under the hood, while on the opposite
side two young men dressed as Swiss guards
took their seats. Soon the parade began to move,
first around the square and then to the club.
I began to feel sick. The gas or the smoke from
the torches was suffocating me. I repented of
ever having come. I longed for my father and
mother. I wished I were at home or in school.
I did not know where my aunt and Gizelda
were. If only I were with some of my friends,
and not with these strangers! I began to worry
about the polonaise that my aunt had mentioned. I did not know how I should get out
of that.

Arriving at the club, those in fancy dress began
to enter, circling the great hall. I sought anxiously to see a face I would recognize. At one
end the queen was enthroned. Now it was time
for the couples to form for the polonaise. I felt

great anguish; and without realizing it, I cried out in the depths of my soul: "My New Friend!" As if in answer, I heard someone say, "Senhorita." Turning around, I saw before me a man dressed as a Domino, with a black satin costume and a half mask of black velvet. He presented himself as my partner saying: "Senhorita, let us take our places for the polonaise."

I tried to excuse myself, saying: "I have never taken part in the polonaise; for up to now, I have not made my debut as a young woman." (I said this because I understood that only young women should take part in the polonaise and dance with the young men.) "I do not know how to dance the polonaise or to do any dance. I only know the simple dances that Acácia taught me."

The black Domino laughed heartily at this and answered: "Senhorita, do not be afraid of making a mistake. I shall be your guide, and I consider it a great honor to be your first dancing master."

The music had begun and the couples began to file by. My steps were uncertain and awkward. I felt outside my field. However, my unknown teacher encouraged me with his smoothness and easy manner. At a certain point in the dance, when we were entering the second hall, the partners separated. Losing confidence in myself, I left the line of dancers and began to look anxiously at all the faces in the hall, hoping to see my aunt or Gizelda. But once more I saw coming toward me my partner, who had won my confidence.

I felt relieved and happy that this unknown man was my friend. He offered me his arm, saying: "I shall accompany you; I am your partner." I answered: "I have not yet seen my aunt or Gizelda, and I wish to be with them."

"What are their costumes?"

"One is dressed as a Norwegian, and the other as a student."

"Ah! I saw them," said my partner; "they were leaving in their car for the Club Jaguarense."

I could have wept when I heard this. I felt myself alone and abandoned. My partner added: "I will take you to the Jaguarense. Do not worry!" This made me very happy, and I did not know how I could thank my kind partner. "Yes, yes," I said, "please take me to the Jaguarense. I do not want to stay here."

"Wait here for me," he then said, "while I go for my car." I waited in the balcony of the club. In a few minutes my partner returned, saying: "Let us go, Senhorita!" We walked through the first hall as the orchestra was playing and the couples dancing. When we arrived at the main door that opened out on the long row of marble steps leading down to the street, my partner offered me his hand. At the same instant I felt my left hand grasped by another hand, the hand of my New Friend.

Immediately I remembered that terrifying scene of 1905 in the square in Santa Vitória. I thought of the big masked man with the flashing eyes, who had also taken me by the hand. Frightened, I looked at the face of my partner, which was covered with a half mask of velvet. His eyes were flashing in the same way. His gloved hand grasped mine, pulling me forcefully now and trying to make me descend the steps. But the holy hand of my New Friend held me back. The scene of 1905 was reproduced in this scene of 1915. The black Domino now filled me with fear. His eyes looked fearsome behind his mask. His hand, enclosed in a black kid glove, tried to drag me along; yet he could not do so. The holy hand of my New Friend held me firm, gently but strongly. Then the black Domino spoke, not now in the smooth tones of a polished gentleman: "Let's go and quickly!" He gave me a strong pull in an effort to drag me from where I stood, but he was unsuccessful. Uttering some phrase, he freed me and ran down the steps, disappearing in the street.

The holy hand of my New Friend now rested gently and compassionately upon my shoulder. I looked at his holy face and there perceived that "sweetness" which constituted my delight. I returned calmly to the hall and saw my aunt looking for me. Then a man dressed as a tourist invited me to be his partner in the quadrille. My grandmother, who was also present, told me to accept. The tourist was not wearing a mask. I took my place, and—let the great and merciful fidelity of my New Friend be exalted here—he, a prince of Heaven, the holy messenger of the most high God, took his place in the quadrille beside his little friend, the miserable creature whom it was his duty to protect and guide.

When the quadrille was finished, my partner brought me back to my grandmother. On the following days I had no desire to go to the dances at night. I only went in the afternoon to the parade, but no black Domino approached me.

*   *   *

O MY New Friend, thy fidelity and love certainly saved me once again from some great evil, of which I do not know even to this day. Amen.

Chapter 19

Studies and Examinations

AT THE beginning of the school year in 1915 my father greatly encouraged me in my studies. He always showed the greatest interest in the good marks I obtained in deportment and application to study. The tri-monthly report cards were read by my father and studied by him. These report cards were blue in color and contained the marks of the student in all the subjects in her course of study. At the bottom of the card was given the average mark, obtained by adding all the marks and dividing them by the number of subjects. Upon this average mark depended the high or low place that the student obtained in the class.

My father was supremely happy whenever he could read on the blue report card: "First Place." Then he rejoiced; my mother was pleased, and I was immensely happy. Nearly always, however, I obtained only second place. Just twice did I obtain the first. There was in the class a girl whom we shall call Elena. She was so talented, studious and good that she always deserved and won first place. When I did obtain the first place, it was only by sharing the honors with Elena, for we both had the same marks on those two occasions.

At the beginning of the first tri-monthly period that year my father said to me: "If you win first place, you will make your father very happy and I shall give you a beautiful present."

"I shall obtain it," I answered, "no matter how much I have to study. You will see 'First Place' written on my report card." I bent all my endeavors to this end. I studied constantly and perseveringly. I always had my lessons well prepared. There was not one question in any subject that I feared. Every day before beginning my studies I asked with great devotion the help of my New Friend. At school I paid visits to the image of Our Lady and made novenas that I might obtain first place. I wanted above all to please my father rather than to obtain the present he had promised me. For I loved my father very much, and to give him pleasure was of much more importance to me than to obtain all the presents in the world, no matter how beautiful they might be.

Toward the end of the three months I knew the answers to all the questions in each subject and I had not the slightest fear of failing. I should certainly share first place honors with Elena. Neither she nor Sister Clementina nor my father knew of the intense efforts I had applied to my studies.

History: The Trojan War

One morning, however, I awoke with a fever and I had to remain in bed. I had the mumps. I lost two weeks of class. Naturally I got behind in my lessons. When I returned to school, I had to study doubly hard, catching up on the lessons I missed and learning the new lessons. Examinations were only a few days away. I studied and studied once more, until I seemed to have everything in hand again. There were sixteen questions in World History. I had all of them on the tip of my tongue with the exception of the question on the Trojan War. I remember this so well. It was impossible for me to study this question thoroughly. There was not enough time. I was exhausted, and the answer was so long. I thought: "Now, I know perfectly the answers to fifteen questions. Perhaps the examination question will be on the Trojan War! No! My New Friend and Our Lady will not permit that."

The day for the examination in World History arrived. I had done so well in the other examinations that I was certain I would share first place honors. I had studied the question on the Trojan War, but it was so long that I could not retain it in my head. I remembered only—because it was interesting—the story of the big wooden horse within which the Grecian soldiers had hidden.

The hour for the examination arrived, and we gathered around Sister Clementina's desk to draw out of a box the particular question that each one had to answer. I placed my hand in the box and trembling I drew out a question. Unfolding the paper, I read: "The Trojan War." I felt lost, woebegone, victimized. Then someone began to pull my dress. It was another student, trembling and nervous like myself. "Let us exchange questions," said she. "I know the Trojan War much better than the one I drew on the Wars of the Medes."

"Ah!" I thought, "I know that question well enough to obtain a hundred. That would save my record." At the same moment, with the quickness of lightning, more rapid even than thought—for I had not even time to think over the proposition made to me—I felt on my shoulder the holy hand of my New Friend. Then I was able to think clearly: "What kind of a proposition is this? It would be cheating. Better to obtain zero than to win one hundred percent by cheating." I answered the other student: "No! Sister Clementina would be deceived. You know your question much better than I know mine."

Then the Sister gave the signal and we went to our places. Elena won first place in the class. I obtained only fourth place, for I had written nothing about the Trojan War except a few lines that I remembered here and there. The Trojan War spoiled my report card. I got zero in World

History. When with sinking heart I showed my report card to my father, the holy hand of my New Friend rested on my shoulder. I did not receive the present from my father, but the "sweetness" on the holy face of my New Friend meant much more to me than the richest presents in the world. My father did not have the happiness of seeing me win first place that time, but afterward I gave him this pleasure several times, when Elena had departed for Cruz Alta.

The Magic Pillow

The incident I am now going to narrate will show how simple and foolish I was, how slow was my intelligence, how incapable I myself was of accomplishing any good work, no matter how small it was, without the help of my New Friend.

One morning during the school year of 1916 Alice said to me at recreation: "Let us go to the club this afternoon at four o'clock, and from the balcony we can watch the Scout parade." I answered regretfully: "What a shame the parade is marked for that hour! It will continue until dark, and then I shall not have time enough for studying. I have an enormous amount to study in literature, catechism and geography. It will take me two hours to learn this matter."

Alice insisted, saying: "And will you fail to go to see the Scout parade just because of your lessons? You are really childish. I have to study just as much as you, but I do only the written lessons. I never study the others. At night when I go to bed, I place the book containing the next day's lesson under my pillow. Then on the following day in class I have the whole lesson on the tip of my tongue."

My surprise knew no bounds, and in my wondering admiration I asked her: "Then why is it that sometimes you do not know the lesson?" Alice answered promptly: "Because I did not place the book beneath the pillow." She continued: "Experiment for yourself today. Tonight when you go to bed place the catechism, with the literature and geography books, under your pillow! Tomorrow you will know the lessons better than you have ever known them in your life. I give you my guarantee."

I did not know how to answer her, so great was my admiration. Here was I spending every afternoon studying, when I had such a simple means at my disposal. I thanked Alice from my heart, and promised to give her the most beautiful collection of holy cards that I possessed. I was radiant with happiness. I could now go to the Scout parade. Before we parted we arranged that Alice would call for me at four o'clock and that I would be ready to leave immediately.

That afternoon everything went off splendidly. From the balcony of the club we watched the Scouts parading. After the parade had ended we went riding with Isabel and Laura in their automobile. When the strident whistle of the electric light plant announced the hour for lighting the streets, Isabel and Laura took me home. I felt so happy. I had enjoyed myself the whole afternoon, and on the following day I would know my lessons better than I ever did. I went to my box of holy cards to take out the collection that I had promised Alice. With my heart full of joy and gratitude I prepared the little package in the best manner possible, using the finest paper and tying it with a ribbon.

At bedtime, completely convinced of what Alice had told me and in the most sincere good faith, without having read even once the lessons for the following day, with a happy heart I placed carefully under the pillow the catechism, the literature book and the geography book. A short while after retiring, I fell asleep, dreaming of great triumphs on the following day.

The next morning I took the books from beneath the pillow. So firm was my conviction that I did not even look at the lessons, nor did I remember to try to see whether I had absorbed the lessons during the night. Very pleased with myself, I set out for school, taking with me the present for Alice as proof of my gratitude. When I entered the classroom, it was still a little early and Alice was not there. Soon she entered the classroom and looked around for me. I pointed quietly to the package I had brought her. Sister Clementina gave the signal for prayer and the class began.

The first class was in religion. At the first question all raised their hands to answer. But I perceived that I did not know the answer to that question. With the second question it was the same, and the same with the third. I need not describe my disillusionment. I sought to look at Alice. She had her hand raised to answer, and she was looking at me and smiling ironically. Soon it was my turn to be called upon. Confused and miserable, I stood up. I could not answer one word. I lowered my head and only by a violent effort was I able to restrain the tears that wanted to burst forth.

Sister Clementina asked me if I were ill. I shook my head to signify that I was not. Then Alice was asked the question which I failed to answer. She answered it perfectly. My feeling of disillusionment increased. But I still did not understand the reason for my failure. For up to that moment in my sixteen years of life, I had never thought that anyone would deceive another, even for fun. Whenever my eyes sought Alice's, she turned her head toward me and smiled ironically. The class in religion came to an end. The bell for recreation sounded. After recreation we would have classes in literature and in geography.

In an effort to solve the puzzle, I thought: "I should have opened the books when I placed

them under the pillow, but I left them closed."
I had been in doubt about this the previous
night. Sister Clementina now gave the signal to
leave the classroom. I placed carefully in my
pocket the package of holy cards. In the school-
yard, as soon as we received the signal of dis-
missal, Alice came running toward me, laughing
uncontrollably. Still far from guessing the truth,
I was to suffer another disillusionment. With
the package of holy cards in my hand and with
my heart oppressed by the tears I was forcing
back, I waited to hear what Alice would say. I
was certain she would explain my failure by saying the books should have been left open. Opening her mouth to speak, Alice exclaimed: "I
never thought you were so childish. Did you
really place the books under the pillow and do
no studying? What a story you swallowed! You
are really a simpleton."

At these words the veil finally fell from before
my eyes, and I understood everything. Alice had
deceived me. Immediately there was a strong
reaction in me. In an instant, a multitude of
thoughts began to run through my mind: "Alice
has told me a lie, and now she is making fun
of me. Humiliated and angry, I now keep back
the tears through self-love. Alice must not see
me crying. But she is laughing, and laughs still
more when she sees the package I have in my
hand."

And now Alice said: "But I do not give up

my right to the holy cards you promised me."

On hearing this piece of sarcasm I could not contain myself any longer. I was about to say to her: "If these were not holy cards I would tear them in a thousand pieces and throw them in your face as testimony of my contempt." But these words did not leave my mouth. Before I had time to say them, the holy hand of my New Friend rested gently on my shoulder and I understood that he wished me to offer the package to Alice. Using a violent effort to subdue my self-love, I offered the package and Alice accepted it. Still laughing, she thanked me sarcastically. Perhaps she thought it was all a joke and did not understand how she had pierced my heart.

When we returned to class, I had the same experience with literature and geography as with catechism. However, this time the "sweetness" of my New Friend consoled my soul and I did not suffer any more. Sister Clementina only said: "Cecy is sick today. We shall leave her alone." After that she did not call on me.

That same afternoon, by way of exception, I related to my father and mother what had happened, omitting some of the details. My father smiled at the story, but afterward he said to me very seriously: "My child, since you are sixteen years old you cannot be entirely blameless." My mother added: "She's a simpleton. She believes everything that is said to her. If someone said to her: 'Throw yourself into this well head first and you will arrive at the bottom without bruising even a finger,' very probably she would believe it."

As for myself, I was embarrassed and ashamed to realize that I had been so foolish. Yet it seems that this incident did not serve as a lesson for me, as I continued to be just as foolish. I narrate this incident only to show how hard my Guardian Angel had to work to protect his little friend from her own foolishness.

Chapter 20

Threefold Censorship

IN THE same year of 1916 a famous operetta company came to Jaguarão. At least it was advertised widely as such. This company also staged dramas. Before this company arrived, an agent came to Jaguarão to find out if the town could support such a group of great artists. The company was to play in the Theater Esperança. The agent went from house to house selling reservations for all the shows that the company would stage in Jaguarão. My father did not wish to take reservations for all the shows, for he said that the admission charge was very high. A box for five people cost two hundred cruzeiros. He said "Perhaps we can go to one or the other."

At the Theater

The company finally arrived, and that afternoon the artists, dressed in all their finery, paraded through the streets in a long line of automobiles with the hoods down. Sunday was the day of their first show. On returning from Mass I received a card from Anna inviting me to see the show from the box which her father had reserved. My father and mother gave me permission, and that evening I waited in happy anticipation for Anna to come. Soon she arrived, and we set off for the theater. The theater was filled to overflowing. Every box was occupied, and every seat on the main floor was filled. I was seated with Anna and her family in their box.

A small bell tinkled. The company's orchestra began to play selections from the opera *Guaraní* [masterpiece of the Brazilian composer Carlos Gomes]. Then the curtains were drawn aside and the drama began. It was a drama by Alexander Dumas. I do not remember the title. The first scene was set in a luxurious hall in a castle. A nobleman entered and began to speak. That was the end of the drama for me. The holy wings of my New Friend extended themselves before me, as had happened various times, and I neither saw nor heard anything more. A holy "sweetness" bound me, body and soul (I do not know if I can express myself thus). The play came to an end.

On the following day at table my father asked me about the plot of the play. I did not know how to describe it. My mother ridiculed me, calling me a simpleton; but my father, as always, was kind and gentle to me. I wept for the humiliation I experienced. Then my mother comforted me, and so I forgot this whole episode. Later my father reserved a box, but I gave up my place to one of my aunts. My grandmother remained with me that evening. I told my father that I did not like plays, that I liked the circus better. My father smiled and said: "Yes, you certainly have a great liking for the clowns." My father seemed to be resigned to the stupidity of his daughter, but I perceived clearly a certain amount of sadness mixed with that generous resignation.

A Rule for Drinking

The carnival season of 1916 was approaching. In Jaguarão it was the custom to have frequent dances during this season. Groups of boys and girls, dressed usually in Domino costumes, led mock assaults on the clubs or against the homes of different families. These mock assaults were the prelude to dancing. At the time I speak of, the place of assault was the club Jaguarense. Thither went I also, drawn by the enthusiasm of some of my friends.

To speak frankly, I did not have a great liking for dances and for other social gatherings. Certain social customs irritated me. Once, at the birthday celebration of a certain captain, my father said that I embarrassed him. The reason was that when a major offered me champagne for the toast, I told him I did not like it, and he had to go fetch me another beverage. I always liked to say what I thought and to do things that pleased me.

At another gathering a certain doctor was present who liked to pass around the hall speaking in such a learned and high-flown style that I neither understood what he was saying nor did I have any idea of how to answer him. So I said to him: "Would you be so kind as to speak more simply with me? At home my father does not speak to me thus; neither do the Sisters in school." He laughed heartily, saying that I was still a naive young girl. On account of such incidents I began to dislike these social gatherings. I would go to them only when I was caught up by the enthusiasm of others.

But to get back to my narrative. I went to the above dance at the Club Jaguarense, dressed as a Domino in a yellow costume. I was seated with one of my girl friends in the hall when two young men approached us and invited us to dance. I still did not dance well, and I said so to the young man. He, however, said that I danced very well; and he took every dance with me. Only now do I understand that the compliment he paid me was the usual compliment he gave to all his dancing partners. Finally I told him that I was tired and wished to return to my place. Instead, the young man led me to the bar and seated me at one of the unoccupied tables. He called for drinks.

At that moment I would have preferred an ice-cream soda. But remembering the incident of the champagne, I took the drink offered me. Then, this young man, whom I did not know, ordered more drinks. Thinking that I should be lacking in social etiquette if I refused the second drink, I took it and began to raise the glass to my mouth. Before I could taste it, I felt my arm gently secured by the holy hand of my New Friend. My companion began to insist that I take the drink, but through the opposition of my New Friend I understood clearly that I would not be lacking in any social etiquette if I refused. I said: "Thank you, but I am not accustomed to take more than one glass of any beverage." He answered that the glass was very small. However, the holy hand of my New Friend continued to rest on my shoulder.

I am certain that if my New Friend had not prevented me, I would have taken as many glasses as the young man offered me. For I was not thinking of the harm too much drinking would do to me; and on account of what my father had said to me I had an erroneous idea about violating social etiquette by refusing.

My New Friend kept his holy hand upon my shoulder during the time that I remained at the table with that young man. His holy face had a look of placid but sad severity. From this I understood he was displeased with my remaining there with the young man. Therefore, without any explanation, I stood up and told my partner that I was returning to the hall. He wished to accompany me, but I answered that I desired to return alone, and so I did.

✝ ✝ ✳

O MY New Friend, at this moment when I am writing this, I realize that you delivered me from one more evil. You saved your little friend from many evils without her realizing it at the time. Only now do I recall and see from how many dangers and evils you delivered me.

My New Friend, I still love you much, in spite of your having hidden yourself and having left your weak friend as if abandoned. But I know well that you do this because Our Lord wills it. Therefore I also will it, and confide always in your protection. Amen.

An Improper Book

In the year 1916 the Ginásio Espírito Santo was closed in Jaguarão and the members of the teaching community were transferred to Jaú in the State of São Paulo. Soon thereafter I felt the great loss of my spiritual director, Canon Godofredo Evers. Ever since I was ten years old I had been accustomed to his spiritual direction. Each week he laid out the spiritual program I was to follow.

In the year 1917 a new phase began in my life. I became subject to violent scruples over the least action that I judged I had done badly. For a long time I suffered this cruel torment.

However, I had a great love for Our Lord, Our Lady and my New Friend, and my conscience never accused me of being unfaithful to their inspirations—I mean voluntarily unfaithful. This was an extraordinary grace of my God. Horror for sin increased considerably in my soul. I believe that it was through this that I was able to pass unharmed over the difficult phase of my girlhood. During the hours of leisure on holidays and holydays, in order to alleviate the battle going on in my soul, I began to devote myself to reading.

There was a library at the school, and every Saturday we could take out a book that was to be returned on Monday. Until his departure it was Padre Godofredo who chose the book I was to read. Oftentimes he spoke during the meetings of the Children of Mary on the danger of bad books. He instilled in me such a fear of bad reading that if an unfamiliar book should fall into my hands I would be incapable of leafing through it unless circumstances obliged me to do so. But at the time I am speaking of, I missed the judgment of my faithful spiritual director.

I was even wary of the books in the school library. Once another student recommended to me a book in our school library entitled *The Great Sinner (Magna Peccatrix)*, but Padre Godofredo said to me: "That book is not bad, but I do not want you to read it, either now or later."

Twice that book fell into my hands, but thanks to the grace of God, I did not even open it. On Saturdays I would go to the school library and ask for the list of books. Then I would ask my New Friend to choose a book for me. Without anyone perceiving me I would close my eyes and choose the book on which I placed my finger in the list.

One Saturday the librarian could not attend to us and I had no book to read. I was disgusted. Arriving home, I felt the need of something to read. Then I remembered one of my friends who liked to read and who always had many books. I sent a note to her, asking her to choose an interesting book for me and to send it to me. In my anxiety to obtain a book I forgot my fear. I did not even think about the possibility of getting a bad book. Soon I received a beautiful new volume entitled *The Vestal Virgins (As Vestais)*.

I had the custom of reading in my room; so, very happy with my good fortune, I betook myself thither. Seating myself, I took the book in my hands. As I began to open the book to the first page, the holy hand of my New Friend rested on mine, so that the book closed of itself and fell to the ground. I looked at his holy face, and it was sad and severe. I understood: I should not read that book.

A great repentance filled my soul for having taken, for the first time, a book without consulting beforehand my New Friend, as had been my custom since the departure of Padre Godofredo. I knelt down and asked pardon of Our Lady and my New Friend. I wept tears of true repentance. After a few moments, while I was resting my head on the bed as I wept, I felt once more the holy hand of my New Friend gently resting upon me. I was so accustomed to my Guardian Angel that I understood from this that he was again pleased with his poor repentant friend. His holy face was no longer sad. He was my heaven here.

With closed eyes I picked up the book. Wrapping it, I sent it back to my friend, telling her frankly that I remembered I could not read any book without the permission of my Father-confessor.

Chapter 21

My Father and I Saved from Dangers

MY FATHER was still in the military colony of the Upper Uruguay. In that colony there were no houses of permanent material. Before he was sent there, the government ordered a house made of finished wood. This was furnished for him. Since we remained in Jaguarão, my father lived alone except for a cook, another servant who took care of the house, and a baggageman. I have described already how greatly I missed my father, whose memory was always with me. In my loneliness over the absence of my father, many times I worried about him, thinking that he would not have anyone to take good care of him when he was sick.

On those days when I had not made some "big" sacrifice for my father, I could not sleep at night until I had said five decades of the Rosary for him. My last petition to my New Friend before falling asleep was invariably this: "O my New Friend, as soon as I fall asleep, please go to my father and remain watching over him, together with his New Friend." Only then was I able to sleep in peace.

A Fire at Night

One day I was more lonely than usual on account of my father's absence. I kept making little sacrifices for him and I offered up more than one Rosary to Our Lady for him. I longed to see him. I thought only of him. That night I asked my New Friend to go to my father even before I went to sleep. When it was late and all were asleep, I awoke thinking of my father. It was the middle of winter. Since I could not sleep any more, I thought I would say the Rosary for my father. I remained in bed because the cold discouraged me from arising and kneeling down.

I began the first mystery of the Rosary, but I had not said three *Hail Marys* when a strong impulse impelled me to get up, filling my mind with the thought that I must pray on my knees. I knelt down at the foot of the bed and prayed with the greatest devotion that my soul was capable of. I was most firmly convinced that my father needed my prayers. I said not only five mysteries of the Rosary, but also on every bead of my rosary I said the prayer, "Remember that I belong to thee." Then I began to say the prayer to my Guardian Angel on every bead.

Up to this time my New Friend had not manifested himself. I was not surprised by this, because I had asked him to go to my father. On finishing the rosary of prayers to my Guardian Angel I began to say the *Glory Be to the Father* on my beads, for I was still filled with the strong desire to pray, in spite of the bitter cold, the darkness and the silence. At the end of ten *Glory Be to the Fathers*, I felt gently resting on my head the holy hand of my New Friend, as if he wished to say to me: "Enough, your father is safe." At least I was convinced of this. I returned to bed, and a short time afterward, in the most holy peace, I fell asleep.

Some days went by, and then my mother received a long letter from my father, containing some clippings from a newspaper which related the following story. My father had imprisoned a soldier for committing a fault against discipline. When the period of his sentence was up, this soldier was placed at liberty. Two or three nights after being freed, and exactly on the night when I had awakened to pray, my father had been awakened by the noise of loud crackling in the house. He saw himself surrounded by a fiery brightness. Seeing that the house was on fire, he leaped out of bed. He wanted to go into the next room to save important papers, but it was impossible. The flames were devouring everything. He tried to go through the other door leading out of his room, but this, too, was barred by the leaping flames.

He ran then to the window, but the heat of

the fire had warped the wood and he could not open it. Suddenly, however, there was a loud roaring of the fire and the window opened. The flames were already licking the window frame as my father scrambled through to safety. My father then gave the signal of alarm, which brought help. Investigations were made and the cause of the fire was discovered. The soldier who had been imprisoned had set fire to the house out of vengeance. He himself confessed this afterward.

I have narrated this incident, because I am firmly convinced that it was my New Friend who saved my father. I believe that it was he who opened the window so that my father could escape. I did not tell anyone that I prayed those holy Rosaries on the night of the fire. (Such was my custom, although I cannot explain it.) I know only that my New Friend left me praying while he went to save my father; and when he placed his holy hand on my head, my father was already saved.

*   *   *

O MY New Friend, may the good God be glorified in thy holy fidelity! Amen.

A Drunken Visitor

A year after the fire in the military colony the government withdrew the military and sold that whole region to settlers. My father was then transferred to Pôrto Alegre, but we still remained in Jaguarão. Every night it was my mother's custom to visit our grandmother after supper. My brothers always went with my mother while I remained at home with Acácia, Conceição and Abelino, the soldier whom my father had brought from Santa Vitória. I always had many lessons to study, for I was very slow in my studies and the whole afternoon was not enough for me.

This evening I speak of was in the summertime. I was studying on the big veranda in front, which opened off the entrance. Everything was open, the gate leading off the street and the door leading on to the veranda. I was studying at the head of the long table that was in the center of the veranda. I was lonely for my father. In spite of his frequent journeys I could not accustom myself to his absence. Every now and again I would look toward the easy chair in one of the corners of the veranda where, if he were home, my father would be keeping me company, reading the newspapers. Then I would be filled with a longing to see my father

I was studying alone. In such circumstances my New Friend did not manifest himself. However, I felt him always at my side. I rarely changed my place. Whenever my father was not in the house, if my mother left to visit our grandmother, she would tell Abelino not to leave the house but to remain with me, Acácia and Conceição. Abelino was always at the back of the house, and at that time of the evening he was usually filling the barrel and large pitchers with water. Acácia and Conceição were putting the kitchen in order.

So absorbed was I in my studies that someone came up on the veranda unnoticed by me and stood opposite the table. When I raised my eyes, I was terrified to see a man standing in front of the table. My voice froze in my throat and my body seemed to become paralyzed. I wanted to scream and flee, but I could not do so. The man appeared to be drunk, for he supported himself by holding on to the table with his two hands. He was dressed in the garb of a southern Brazilian cowboy. He was tall and strong, but his face was evil-looking and his eyes appeared somewhat like those of an idiot. Attached to the wide belt around his waist, I saw a sheath with a knife.

I cannot say how long the man remained looking at me and I at him, but it was a very short interval. Then he began to come toward me, around the table, still supporting himself on it. He said in the Spanish of the Uruguayan frontier: "If you speak a word, I will choke you." Terror overwhelmed me, and only by a strong effort could I whisper, "My New Friend." Immediately his holy hand rested on my shoulder. The terror that had frozen my faculties disappeared as if by a charm. I stood up to go and call Acácia. Then the man fled, overturning a chair in his hasty exit.

I stopped, therefore, and looked at the holy face of my New Friend. It had a look of severity. Ah, then I understood and realized my fault. Soon after my mother had departed I had asked Abelino to buy some chocolate for me. He had refused me in a roundabout way, saying that he must remain in the house while my mother was absent. But I was not accustomed to being refused; so I insisted and offered him many reasons why he should go, saying that it was still early, that my mother would not mind, that the shop was close by and that he could go quickly. Finally this good man went, although he did not want to do so. By the time he returned the intruder had already fled.

I did not tell Abelino what had happened, not, thanks be to God, because I wished to hide my fault, but because he was always so faithful in the fulfillment of his duties that his conscience would accuse him excessively of being to blame, while it was I who was really the culprit. Then again, my mother would scold him.

When Abelino returned I felt twice as sorry for my fault, for when he handed me the packet of chocolate, he said: "I practically ran there and back; I was so worried. Do not ask me to do this any more! For I should not deserve the confidence that your mother has in me." I could scarcely restrain the tears that tried to burst forth. I could only say: "Thank you, Abelino." I did not touch the chocolate. On the following day I tried to give it to Abelino, but he would not accept it. Then I gave it to Acácia and Conceição.

On the night of the intrusion I did not take tea, as was my custom, but retired early. Before retiring, in sincere repentance I asked pardon of Our Lord and my New Friend. They always forgave me. I wept with repentance. When the tears had stopped, I looked at the holy face of my New Friend, and thereon I perceived that "sweetness" which made me forget everything and filled me with true peace. On the next day, not waiting for Saturday, I went with another student after school to the parish church, where I made my Confession. Our Lord forgave me. The only ones who knew of this incident were Our Lord and my New Friend and, here on earth, my Father-confessor.

Miguel

In the year 1918 my father went to Rio de Janeiro, while we remained in Jaguarão. Much more than on other occasions, although I was now eighteen years old, I felt the absence of my father. I declare with complete conviction that I should not have been able to bear the loneliness I felt because of my father's absence were it not that principally on those occasions I felt vividly with me the presence of Our Lord and my New Friend.

My father was for me a second New Friend, one who was visible. When I was sick and my father was home, he did not stir from my bed. At the side of my bed he placed his easy chair, and there my "visible New Friend" remained, giving me my medicine and tasting my food to see if it was properly prepared. On account of this, it is easy to understand the great and practically unbearable loneliness I felt when he was absent.

My father remained in Rio for several months. His first months there passed by without incident. He was staying in a hotel. With punctual regularity my mother received letters from him. Then there was a long interval without any letter. Finally we received a telegram from him, saying that he was sick but that there was no cause for fear.

And now, just as on the night of the fire in the military colony, I would pray every night after the lights had been extinguished. Getting up, I would kneel at the foot of the bed while I said a Rosary to Our Lady; then a rosary of the prayer "Remember that I belong to thee"; and another of the prayer to my Guardian Angel, until his holy hand rested on my shoulder to tell me that it was enough.

This was the invariable scene every night.

When I began my prayers, I asked my New Friend to go to my father. My holy and most faithful Angel never denied the petition of his little friend. Every night he went to visit my father while I remained praying. He announced his return by placing his holy hand on my shoulder. Only then could I sleep.

This is what befell my father. One afternoon as he was returning to his hotel on a trolley car, he began to feel sick. On arriving at the hotel, he told the room attendant that he felt sick and asked him to call a doctor. At that time the first cases of the terrible Spanish epidemic were beginning to appear in Rio. This had been unknown in Rio up to that time, and my father was one of the first victims. He became critically ill and was very close to death.

My mother's telegrams were answered by the room attendant. For years afterward my father never ceased to recall and proclaim the honor, dedication and fidelity of this simple hotel room attendant, to whom my father was a complete stranger. Even to the present time I have kept his name in my heart. His name was Miguel. I did not know him, but I have full certainty that my New Friend availed himself of his services. And now I see with holy joy that this good youth possessed the same name, Miguel, as my New Friend. At that time I did not know both had the same name.

In that section of apartments where my father

was staying there were twenty-four deaths. When this terrible epidemic was at the height of its fury, doctors were hard to find and the few nurses available were paid enormous sums to take care of patients during the night. Through it all Miguel cared for my father as if he were his own parent. The least thing was never lacking to my father. When the first doctor became sick with the disease, Miguel brought a second. When he, too, fell sick, Miguel brought a third, and a fourth, and a fifth. How I enjoyed hearing my father praise the good Miguel!

Months after the outbreak of this epidemic my father was convalescing. He was so weak that he could not even sit up in bed without being helped, but Miguel was always there. When my father became stronger and was ready to descend to the garden to take the sun, it was Miguel who helped him down and back. I beg the reader's pardon if I seem to dwell too much on describing all that Miguel did for my father, but I feel a holy enthusiasm when I speak of that good youth. I admired that remarkable soul, and I felt a holy love, a love of gratitude and admiration, in my own soul whenever my father spoke to me of him. I never saw my father weep, not even at the death of my sister Dilsa. Yet every time I heard him speak of Miguel I seemed to see tears glistening in his eyes.

When my father had completely recovered his health and was able to travel, he made ready to return to Jaguarão. I remember well how my father described his departure in the following words: "That simple young man, with a bearing so humble, hid within himself a great soul, an ideal heart, a character of steel. His presence always inspired respect and admiration in me, an old soldier who always strove to maintain purity of conscience and to ennoble my character. Miguel never accepted anything for his services. I told him that although my fortune consisted of the modest salary of an official of the army, yet on that occasion I could afford to give him a certain sum. But Miguel sincerely refused to accept anything."

My father, being deeply moved and desiring to show his gratitude, took the ring from his finger and offered it to Miguel, asking him not to refuse it. It was in vain. Miguel said to my father: "You have a family. Offer it to one of your daughters and I shall consider myself doubly repaid."

This was what my father did as soon as he arrived home. Calling me, he placed the ring on my finger, saying: "My daughter, I want to fulfill the wish of the best friend I ever had in this world, the most noble and most honorable man that I have ever met in my life." Then my father told me of the most kind and edifying deeds of Miguel. In spite of not knowing him I conceived a true esteem of his character. From that moment forward, I was convinced that the good Miguel certainly maintained some relation with my New Friend.

At this moment, when I am writing these pages, I am more convinced. Miguel was the name of that good youth, and today I know that Miguel is also the name of my New Friend. Many times my father wrote to Miguel, but he never had the happiness of receiving an answer. My father told me, further, that when he went on longer walks with Miguel through the park, Miguel was always very reserved and discreet when my father interested himself in his welfare, seeking to find out something about his family, his resources, his life. My father never learned anything more about this young man except his name. Whenever my father ended up telling me something about Miguel, he always added: "A soul chosen for great things!" However, I never understood this exclamation of my father.

Chapter 22

The Temptation of Beauty

TOWARD the end of the year 1918, my last year in my beloved Immaculate Conception College, the parochial branch of the Children of Mary resolved to organize a festival to benefit the Working Girls' Society of St. Elizabeth. They asked our school branch of the Children of Mary to help them. They decided to give a presentation of the play *Miriam*. Reverend Mother Susanna granted the use of the college theater. Rehearsals were under the direction of Dona Isaura Vargas (today Sister Núncia), who was a teacher in the primary school and stayed at the college.

I was chosen for a part in this play. The part given to me was that of Cornelia, a Roman lady of fascinating beauty. I accepted the part very naturally, without remembering that I was plain-looking and without thinking how I could be transformed into a fascinating beauty.

Another character in the play was Faustina, also a Roman lady. She was a sister of Cornelia but not noted for her beauty. This part was given to another student, who was really beautiful and had all the qualities necessary to play the part of Cornelia. I do not know why there was this seeming mistake in casting. The part of Cornelia was given to me, who was really plain-looking and ungraceful. The girls in charge of the festival were the ones who gave out the parts, beginning with Dona Isaura, who took the part of Gideon, a young Israelite. But the point is that I did not even think about any unsuitability in the casting. Very pleased, I accepted my part, which was an important one, and I began to study my lines for the first rehearsal.

At home I told my father and mother of the part I had in the play, and I described the plot for them. My father, who was always most interested in everything that concerned us, listened to me without interrupting. Then he read every line of my part. At the end he said: "The play seems very beautiful, but it seems to me also that those in charge of the festival did not assign the parts to the proper players, at least, not your part. The Roman lady Cornelia was very beautiful and also very proud. As such, she dominated everyone. My child, you cannot interpret this part, and on account of that you will not please the public."

Only then, when I heard my father's words, did I make a comparison between myself and the part I was to play. I knew very well that I was not beautiful. I even considered myself ugly. Knowing that my father was right, as always, I answered him: "Yes, father, it's true. This drama would turn into a comedy in the scene where the young Israelite proclaims the alluring beauty of the daughter of the Roman senator. What a disappointment for the audience when, instead of a Roman beauty, they would see appearing on the stage an ugly little lady!" My father began to laugh. Then pulling me toward him, he embraced me, saying: "Tomorrow, give back your part to the girl who gave it to you. Thank her, and explain frankly why you cannot take the part. Then, offer to take another part—for example, that of Euphrosina, or Gideon."

On the following day I did as my father had told me. I went to Dona Honorina, the prefect of the Sodality, who was in charge of the festival, and I explained everything to her. She also laughed heartily and, embracing me, said: "There is no one more responsible for the success of this festival than I. You must look as beautiful as Cornelia. Vicky will take care of your transformation." Then she asked me to keep the part. I promised that I would, on condition, however, that I would not assume any responsibility if Vicky could not make me look beautiful. I referred the whole matter to my father, who finally withdrew his opposition. My mother still offered criticism, saying that she would not go to the play to see "ugly ladies."

The rehearsals went off without difficulty, and soon the time arrived for the dress rehearsal.

Vicky lent me the beautiful dress she wore as Queen of the last carnival in the Club Jaguarense. It was truly beautiful. The girls arranged the long cloak of velvet and ermine according to the Roman custom. I had everything else I needed—rings, bracelets for the arms and for the wrists, a beautiful diadem of pearls, and long earrings according to the Roman fashion. On my feet I wore sandals of white satin, trimmed in gold.

Vicky, who had much experience in the art of beautifying others, assumed the task of making me look beautiful. She twisted and wound my hair on top of my head, imitating a picture of the Roman coiffure. Finally I was ready. The other actresses and the girls thought I looked "beautiful." They brought me a mirror and I was satisfied with my supposed beauty. I hardly recognized myself. Was it really I? My face was hidden under a veritable camouflage of painting—lily water, rouge, blue pencilling under the eyes, lipstick and all the other cosmetics that Vicky had at her disposal.

I heard so much about how beautiful I looked that, peering at myself again in the mirror, I thought: "I will buy lily water and all the other things that Vicky used. Then I can always look as beautiful as I do now." I had only conceived this thought when that well-known holy hand of my New Friend rested on my shoulder. I perceived that his holy face was very sad. Then I understood everything. In the midst of that uproar of voices and laughter, dresses and flowers, actresses being adorned and girls helping them to dress, the murmuring of the audience in the theater and the musicians tuning their instruments—in the midst of all this confusion, the sorrow of great repentance cut through my heart and soul. I had understood that friendly "voice": If I should be as beautiful as I looked then, my soul would be horribly deformed!

"Crazy that I am! Why desire physical beauty, which is purely external, when beauty of soul far surpasses the most dazzling bodily loveliness?" With this thought I had the ardent desire to pull off everything, which now filled me with disgust, to wash off that layer of paint and powder which was only a mask. But this was impossible now. The play was beginning, and my poor soul was oppressed by sorrow, but also—thanks be to God—by the blessed and saving sorrow of repentance. Thanks again to my God and my New Friend, this holy lesson was beneficial. Never again did I have occasion to consider myself beautiful, and never more was I anxious about being beautiful. Oftentimes I thanked Our Lord for being ugly, because I knew that if I were beautiful my soul would be ugly.

One or two weeks after the night of this play Jaguarão received a visit from the Bishop of Pelotas. We repeated this play for His Excellency. However, I refused courageously to have my face painted. I used only a little powder, and that because Sister Clementina told me to do so. It seemed to me that no one thought I was ugly, and His Excellency enjoyed our play. Before the beginning of the play, when I was adorned and dressed up, Dona Honorina brought me the mirror. Then the holy hand of my New Friend rested anew on my shoulder, and his holy face filled my soul with sweetness.

Chapter 23

A Dance in the Country

IN THE year 1919 a certain woman, whom we shall call Dona Sarah, bought a house in our neighborhood in order to pass the winter in town. She was a rancher's wife and spent the summer on the ranch or on a beautiful farm which was about an hour's ride by automobile from the town. We came to know this woman, who was of a friendly and social nature. She was accustomed to give frequent parties at her farm or at the ranch.

In that same year Dona Sarah invited a large number to celebrate the birthday of her son at the farm. We were among those invited. How happy I was on that day! On the road from the town to her farm there was a continuous line of automobiles filled with the guests. We went in the afternoon. At the farm were some country girls who lived there. They had hearts of gold and souls as clear as crystal. I had a great liking for these girls, who were happy and jovial, good and sincere. They had the frankness of children and the morals of saints. They did not have much education and they were bashful. Yet I enjoyed their company.

That night there was a dance, with music furnished by an orchestra from the town. Those girls from the farm were at the dance dressed in their "old-fashioned style," as the town girls considered their dress. Among those country girls was one of about seventeen or eighteen years of age. I do not recall her name any more, but she was a truly good girl. Her mother was dead and she lived on the ranch with her father and an old woman servant. Rarely did she go to the town and she was extremely bashful.

When the dancing began, a young man approached and invited her to dance. She had never danced, but she went out on the floor with her partner. They took a few steps and she was so awkward that everyone began to smile. It is true that her efforts at dancing were funny. Those who did not smile or laugh restrained themselves only out of charity. I immediately remembered the time when I had cut an identical figure at the dance where the black Domino was my partner, when I, too, could dance only a few awkward steps.

Soon the young men from the town saw in this young girl an opportunity to amuse themselves and the crowd. Each one invited her to dance. The simple girl, very pleased with herself, would accept and begin to take her rambling steps. The onlookers would smile and laugh at the girl, who was as pure as an angel. I felt great sorrow and pity for her. By a coincidence she sat beside me at refreshment time. She was delighted with the party and said she was enjoying every minute of the dance.

After refreshments the orchestra leader announced a staff polka. Many couples could take part in this dance, but there had to be a girl or a man without a partner. All took their partners, except one girl, who had none. Now she had to stand in the middle of the hall, holding the staff in her hand and surrounded by the couples. On the signal from the leader, the orchestra began to play and the couples to dance. On a second signal the girl with the staff was to throw it on the floor. Then all the couples had to separate, quickly and keeping in time with the polka. The men went to the right and the girls to the left. The girl who had dropped the staff could go with the girls.

At a third signal the two groups, in marching time, changed sides, the girls going to the right and the men to the left. At the fourth and final signal, the two groups were to unite, and each one was to take the nearest partner. One individual would be left with the staff. During this polka it was always that simple country girl who was left with the staff. She stood red-faced and embarrassed in the middle of the hall while the others smiled and laughed at her.

At the short pause while the groups were changing places, the holy hand of my New Friend descended on my shoulder. His holy face,

looking sad, made me understand that he had
pity for that girl and that he wished me to take
her place. This silent message came as a surprise and a shock. Immediately I felt the unbearable weight of humiliation, vexation and mockery
that would be mine if I were to stand in the
middle of the hall, holding the staff in my hand.
The holy face of my New Friend remained
unchangeable. I cannot describe the enormity
of that sacrifice.

At the final signal from the leader, the two
groups mixed in a quick scramble for partners
while the staff lay on the floor. With excessive
violence I ran toward the staff and grasped it.
No one saw me pick it up, for each one was
intent on getting a partner. When each had
found a partner, I was left alone in the middle
of the hall surrounded by the couples, who were
smiling and laughing. I do not know what kind
of a sorry figure I looked. I know only that the
others laughed at me and that my part was that
of the court jester. I was extremely vexed and
annoyed, but that feeling, too, passed away. At
the end of the polka I dropped the staff. I did
not go any more to the center of the hall,
because with me the staff polka ended. And
there, even in the dance hall, my New Friend
delighted my soul with his holy sweetness.

Chapter 24

The Call to the Religious Life

THE year 1920 was the beginning of my decisions and indecisions about my vocation in life. I had never changed or wavered in the decision I had made on the day of my First Holy Communion, which was afterward confirmed by the explanation of my holy spiritual father. This year, however, brought me real spiritual battles, and I was not able to solve them. There was no one to whom I might have recourse. The Sisters, those holy friends who helped guide the greater part of my childhood and girlhood, were no longer in Jaguarão. The year 1919 was the last year for my beloved Immaculate Conception College, the memory of which I preserve gratefully and clearly in my soul until the present time. Every day I had to fight anew my spiritual battles. Sometimes I made strong resolutions; at other times, I wavered and changed these same resolutions.

I had an intense love for my father, and it seemed to me to be impossible to leave him. I tried to distract my mind from these problems by taking part in amusements and recreation. But the result was the contrary, for in the midst of these my soul felt extreme disgust. If I took part in social festivities, I did so only through social necessity. My father said to me many times: "My child, you must not withdraw from society when it is well ordered according to Christian morals." Since my two sisters were sick, they did not take part in social activities. Always it was I who had to accept the invitations and attend the dances, bazaars, etc. Yet in the midst of these festivities, I suffered bitterly.

About this time two sporting clubs were founded in Jaguarão, the International Sporting Club and the Southern Cross Sporting Club. I received invitations from both to become affiliated with them as a loyal fan or rooter. I decided upon the Southern Cross Club. The enthusiasm of the followers of these two clubs rose to the pitch of delirium. At two o'clock in the afternoon on Sundays, in the football field, the teams of the two clubs played each other. There you could see all the girls and boys of Jaguarão, wearing the colors of their particular club and cheering in exaggerated enthusiasm.

I was swept along on this wave of sporting enthusiasm, and I cheered for the Southern Cross team. One Sunday there was a special game between the champions, the Southern Cross team, and the International Club team. The field was filled to overflowing. All the girls wore the colors of their clubs, and the excitement was intense. My whole being was concentrated on this game. I seemed to forget my anxieties for a very short moment. Then, in the instant when I was most excited and cheering a great goal made by our team, in the midst of that uproar of music, cheers and laughter, I felt lightly, very lightly, on my shoulder that friendly hand. In an instant all the enthusiasm and excitement wearied me; and my soul, suffering in that environment, longed ardently for its ideal.

It was always thus. At the moment when I seemed to enjoy myself in that environment, the holy hand of my New Friend called me back from that useless, petty, tasteless pleasure. In this way, I passed my twentieth and twenty-first years. Then I made a definite decision, but a thousand difficulties stood in the way.*

---

*Sister Maria Antonia wrote the preceding chapter, the last in her autobiography, during the vacation days of December, 1938. Already she was ill and forced to recline in a chair most of the time. Her malady suddenly grew worse and prevented her from continuing the story of her life. She wrote with the sole intention of furnishing her spiritual director and her superiors with information that would enable them to guide her securely in her interior life. A few weeks before her death she asked that her personal notebooks containing her writings be burned since she judged that the information they contained would no longer be "necessary." However, her spiritual director, Father John Baptist Reus, believed that they should be preserved and the account of her life published, as he wisely considered that her life story would be profitable to others.

When Father Reus died in 1947 he left many notes on the mystical life of Sister Maria Antonia. With the help of these notes and information furnished by those Sisters who knew Sister Maria Antonia intimately, the Jesuit priests of Sao Leopoldo are preparing [at the time the present book was first published] a volume that will deal with the young nun's mystical experiences and sufferings. (The life of Father Reus is also of interest for its own sake, particularly to priests. A biographical sketch of Father Reus is to be found in *Revista Eclesiástica Brasileira* published by Editora Vozes Ltda. [Petrópolis, Rio de Janeiro, Brazil] for December, 1951. The author is Padre Fernando Baumann, S.J.)

Appendix

SISTER MARIA ANTONIA'S LIFE IN THE CONVENT

By a Sister Religious

THE reader who has followed attentively the extraordinary story of Sister Maria Antonia's life will want to ask with justified curiosity: "Did not the persons with whom she lived and those who educated her perceive anything of her extraordinary interior life, any one of those marvelous privileges with which God surrounded her childhood and girlhood?" From certain words and attitudes of her spiritual directors, who are now dead, we can deduce that they saw close at hand the work of God in that chosen soul. It was only they, however, who knew. From all others, it seems, God wished to hide everything.

Major João Ludgero de Aguiar Cony and his wife, Dona Antonia Soares Cony, saw with great satisfaction the exemplary conduct of their daughter and her progress in studies. Among her friends and companions, Cecy was always esteemed and well liked because of her affability and constant good humor. For games and pranks they could always count on her, although if they urged her to do something contrary to her obligations, she would refuse immediately and energetically.

She possessed an innate love of truth and justice, allied to an extreme sensitiveness and sense of honor. As a legitimate descendant of the noble military class, she preserved all through her life a notable delicacy in points of honor. Her teachers agree in affirming that she was a model student in every regard, always polite, modest, obedient and diligent. Other than this there was nothing that attracted attention to her person, except her recollection in prayer, her charming naiveness, and her simple and unpretentious manner.

Already in the year 1913 Our Lord had revealed to His little servant that she was to be His spouse. It seems strange, therefore, that Cecy delayed entering the convent; but she did not understand the full meaning of this revelation. The idea of leaving her parents, whom she loved tenderly, did not enter her head at this time. She even thought for a time about marrying, as she saw in this a means of always living close to her beloved parents. For the rest she was accustomed to abandon herself completely to the direction of her Guardian Angel. It was he who took command whenever she was in danger, in order to sustain and keep intact the divine plans for his ward.

When she was eighteen years old, she graduated from her school, which was closed a short

time afterward. The years following her gradu-
ation she passed at home in the exercise of the
profession of private teacher. Some years later,
when the school was reopened by the Franciscan Sisters, Cecy offered her services to them.
Only in 1925 did she realize clearly that God
wished her to enter the religious life without
delay. She did not hesitate any longer. Using
all the forces of her will, she broke the ties that
bound her to her family, even though this caused
her intense suffering. Bidding farewell to her
parents, she followed the call of her Divine
Spouse.

As a Postulant

In June of 1926 Cecy entered as a postulant
the Congregation of Franciscan Sisters whose
provincial house was in São Leopoldo.* Here
she applied herself to acquiring the spirit of St.
Francis of Assisi, which was not difficult for her.
What was more difficult was to live a life so dif-

---

*The title of the Franciscan Congregation to which Sis-
ter Maria Antonia belonged is "The Sisters of St. Francis
of Penance and Christian Charity." This Congregation was
founded in Holland in 1835. This Congregation has also
three Provinces in the United States, where the Sisters are
dedicated to teaching and to hospital work. The mother-
house of the Western Province is at Redwood City, Cali-
fornia; that of the Eastern, at Stella Niagara, New York;
and that of the Midwestern Province at Denver, Colorado.

ferent in form and activity from that which she had passed in her own home. She found it hard to control her natural vivacity and to dominate her strong temperament. The necessity to have patience with her own defects was not easy for her, yet she was not discouraged. Through her love for the holy Franciscan habit, the object of her ardent desires, she declared and showed herself ready for everything.

Only her immediate superiors had knowledge of the marvels that Divine Love was working in her soul. The other members of the religious family noted only her attitude of profound recollection during prayer, the simplicity and frankness of her speech. At recreation she was usually a pleasing conversationalist and knew how to amuse the other postulants with apt jokes and innocent anecdotes.

The day when she would receive the holy habit was approaching. When she was trying on her bridal gown for the ceremony, Our Lord gave her to understand that she would not be among the privileged number who would receive the habit on that day. Her first reaction of disappointment and sorrow nearly prostrated her, but soon she recovered, and from the depths of her soul she said, "Thy will be done." Referring to this, she wrote in 1937: "In Holy Communion, with my heart weighed down with sorrow, I said to Our Lord that He should do with me whatever He willed, provided that I not commit a voluntary sin and that I love Him more and more."

How was that sorrowful prediction to be fulfilled? A short time afterward, on January 18, 1927, Cecy was stricken by the unexpected news of the death of her beloved father. This shock was very great. She became ill and had to rest for some days. On account of the changed circumstances that this brought to her family, serious obstacles arose that prevented her from receiving the religious habit. In fact, she had to leave the convent at this time.

However, Our Lord consoled her in Holy Communion, promising her that she would receive the Franciscan habit one day. That day was not long delayed. She was able to re-enter as a postulant that same year of 1927, on the eve of the feast of the Immaculate Conception. When the postulant's cape was handed to her, her soul was surprised by the sensible presence of Jesus, just as when she received Holy Communion. This grace she enjoyed uninterruptedly for a number of months.

As a Novice and as a Professed Sister

On February 17, 1928, Cecy—now known by her name in religion, Sister Maria Antonia—knelt again at the foot of the altar to receive the white veil of the novice. During her novitiate she happily employed her time in observing the holy rule with great zeal and in seeking to overcome her defects. Deep in the recesses of her soul, Our Lord continued to attract her powerfully to the path of abnegation and sacrifice.

The state of her soul during that period is revealed by the prayer she was accustomed to say daily, following the counsel of her spiritual director: "O my Jesus, do not permit me to be ever ungrateful for the loving thoughtfulness and tenderness with which Thou hast bound me to Thee and obliged me to love Thee. I offer myself to Thee, that I may be deprived of all spiritual consolations and may suffer all the crosses that it pleases Thee to send me. Dispose of me according to Thy Will. I wish and hope to be all Thine. O my Jesus, I love Thee only for Thyself and for nothing more."

This prayer corresponded to the words that she would hear shortly from her Divine Spouse: "You must be a victim of confusion and every kind of contradiction, in reparation for the opposition encountered by My Church. The generosity of a little soul, ignorant of divine things, whose life will be a web of contradictions, will placate My justice." (Cecy was not ignorant of the truths of her religion, but she was completely ignorant of the theory of mysticism.)

On February 14, 1930, when Sister Maria Antonia took her temporary vows, Our Lord made mention anew of sufferings to come. These came that very same year. Those who lived with her knew of the strange sickness that befell her and of the sudden cure that terminated it. No one, however, thought of seeking its cause in mystical trials. Not even the victim herself understood it. About this illness, we now cite some lines which Sister Maria Antonia wrote later on, out of obedience:

"Our Lord did not come in Holy Communion. [By this, she meant that she did not feel the sensible presence of Our Lord in Holy Communion.] From this sprang cruel doubts that filled my soul. I thought that Our Lord was displeased with me. I perceived my New Friend, it is true, but he showed himself disinterested, indifferent to the internal battles that were going on within me. Afterward I felt the most desolate sorrow, which made me suffer so much. It was as if there was an immense vacuum in my soul: the lack, the absence, of my God."

On February 24, 1933, Sister Maria Antonia realized the most ardent desire of her loving heart; she consecrated herself irrevocably to her Divine Spouse by the perpetual vows of poverty, chastity and obedience. With complete dedication and in the spirit of sacrifice she took up anew the profession of teacher in St. Joseph's College in São Leopoldo. (In Brazil, the term *college* embraces primary and secondary schools and teachers' colleges.) She understood admirably her little pupils, who, on their part, admired and loved their kind teacher.

Victim of Divine Love

Shortly her Divine Spouse manifested Himself once more, asking new immolations. After she had obtained permission from the Reverend Mother Provincial, she declared herself ready for everything that Jesus would demand of her, adding, nevertheless, the petition that these trials would not keep her from fulfilling the obligations of the assignment she had received in holy obedience.

Her offering was accepted by Our Lord, who said to her: "My little spouse, I reserve hard trials for thee. The battle will be great. Give me souls, and thy weakness will glorify Me." The Blessed Virgin Mary wished to assure her of her help and protection before the storm of interior abandonment would lay waste her soul. On September 29, 1935, when Sister Maria Antonia was offering insistent prayers to the Mother of Heaven on behalf of immortal souls, the most holy Mother Mary did not hesitate to offer her maternal consolation. Full of concern, she encouraged Sister Maria Antonia for the sacrifice, saying, among other things: "I am the Mediatrix of all graces . . . ; holy desires are accepted by God as reality."

The time of trial soon arrived. Mystical sufferings of soul and body, bringing indescribable sorrows, devastated her soul and mind without pity: sufferings about which St. John of the Cross wrote, saying that they are the vigil of a great feast. For some time Sister Maria Antonia endeavored to hide them, but it did not take long for them to reveal their effects. The members of the community began to notice her, now weighed down by pain, now afflicted by sorrow, at other times restless, sensitive, excitable and even prone to anger. She became a source of puzzlement to the Sisters with whom she lived.

One of her most sorrowful sufferings was the weight of all the sins of the world. She felt the weight of these sins in her soul, as if she herself had committed them, and this feeling plunged her into an abyss of sadness. It is true that from time to time great consolations opened up a bright path through this fearsome blackness of bitter torment, but these lasted only a few hours, or at most, a few days. A day of great peace for her was Easter Sunday in the year 1936. At her request she received from her spiritual director permission to oblige herself to do the most holy Will of God in all things, even in the least actions of her life, under pain of a penance in case of a voluntary infraction. The formula of this promise was found among her writings after her death. It reads as follows:

O MY GOD, today, the day of Thy glorious Resurrection, at this holy Eucharistic moment in which Thou, the great God in all Thy glory, dost lower

Thyself even to me, uniting Thyself so intimately with me: I, Thy little creature, wish to present to Thee my great desire. In the little white Host which I received this moment, I received Thee. O my God, in Thy presence and that of my most holy Mother, of my holy Guardian Angel, of my Holy Father St. Francis, of my holy Patron Saints, St. Anthony and St. Crescentia, and the whole celestial court, I offer Thee my holy vow:

O my God, I promise Thee that I will live, until the last moment of my life, fulfilling Thy most holy Will, even in the least actions. Accept, O my God, through the most pure hands of Thy most holy Mother, this oblation which I offer Thee as a proof of my great love and my great desire to please Thee. Grant me the grace, O Lord, from this moment forward to be able to repeat unceasingly with the holy Apostle: "It is now no longer I that live, but Christ lives in me." (*Gal.* 2:20). For it is the most holy will of God that is acting in His miserable creature. Amen.

The Mystical Espousals

After Holy Communion she fell into an ecstasy. Of this she writes: "Our Lord took me by the right hand and placed a ring on my finger. Then in the center He placed a diamond shining like the rays of the sun; it was Love for the Most Blessed Sacrament. On the left of this He placed another similar diamond: it was Love for the Holy Cross. At the right of the central diamond, He placed another; it was Love for the most holy Will of God. Then Our Lord said: 'My little spouse, I entrust this ring to you. You must guard it well.' This was all. I exulted. I cannot express how much I loved those three diamonds: the sign of my espousals with my God."

The consequence of this vision is highly interesting because it shows the total ignorance of Sister Maria Antonia in mystical theology. When Our Lord counseled her to guard the ring well, she thought within herself: "I shall give it to Reverend Mother Laeta to keep for me."

When she came out of the ecstasy, she was worried because she did not see the ring any more. It was neither on her finger, nor on the bench, nor on the ground, where she looked for it anxiously. As she had to perform her duties toward her students, it was only some hours afterward that she could ask Our Lord about the ring. She did so with many tears, judging that she had lost what Jesus had entrusted to her care. On learning that this ring was not a material one and that this day was a great festival day for her, she burst out with the words: "Great festival? This was a day of great fear for me." But she dried her tears. That whole day and the whole of Easter Monday Our Lord granted her the privilege of perceiving sensibly His holy presence.

These periods of tranquility were rare and

were only a preparation for the most agonizing afflictions. Our Lord condescended to allow His servant to share in the sorrows of His sacred Passion and death on the Cross. The sufferings of Sister Maria Antonia were offered up sometimes in reparation for the persecutions raging against His Holy Church, at other times in expiation for the insults suffered continually by Jesus in the Most Blessed Eucharist. They were offered for the salvation of children, of soldiers, and for the sanctification of the clergy and religious.

The powers of Hell waged a fierce war against her to try to force her to say: "I do not want to suffer more." But as her oath of fidelity she always repeated the ejaculation, "My Jesus, I still love Thee." This was her powerful prayer that drew back souls from the rim of the infernal abyss. This was her cry of victory against the assaults of Hell.

Mission Completed

Toward the end of the year 1938 Sister Maria Antonia became seriously ill. From Our Lord she learned that her mission was nearly completed. Her interior trials terminated. With edifying patience she bore the cruel pains and miseries of her illness. One year before she had renounced voluntarily the "great festival" of her last hour on earth, when she would be filled with heavenly joy by the presence of Jesus, Mary, her Guardian Angel and her holy Patron Saints. All this she had renounced, offering up this sacrifice for a special intention.

Let us now journey in mind to April 22, 1939, the eve of the day set aside as "Priestly Vocation Day." Throughout the archdiocese of Pôrto Alegre, the faithful contested in holy rivalry with one another, seeking to contribute most for this noble and sacred purpose; for this end offering their prayers, sacrifices and donations. It seemed that the last hour of the beloved Sister Maria Antonia had arrived. In the college the Sisters were oppressed by sadness as they sought to prepare for the festival which was to be given for the benefit of the Priestly Vocation Society. Who would not feel sad even in a festive atmosphere, knowing that one of her Sisters was in her death agony?

The last preparations were being made for the festival. The parents of the students had been invited. Then one Sister remembered that the sick Sister had always been noted for her spirit of obedience. She sent a messenger to say to the sick Sister: "Sister Maria Antonia, you cannot take off on your flight to Heaven for a little while longer. How can we conclude preparations for the festival to benefit priestly vocations if we know that you are in your agony?"

Sister Maria Antonia understood the perturbation behind this request. With difficulty she was able to answer in kind words: "I can wait until Monday." Then her death agony ceased. Her sufferings of the following day she offered up generously for the important intentions of the archdiocese. Only after this did her soul take its departure. Her death, on the night of April 24, was serene but wrapped in great suffering, so that, like a faithful image of her Crucified Spouse, she drank to the last drop the chalice of the most bitter suffering.

The surviving members of her family mourned deeply the premature passing of Sister Maria Antonia. Her students wept over their loss. Her Sisters in religion were grief-stricken by the departure of a beloved member of their community. The students hastened to write tender notes containing requests and recommendations, which were placed with the body in the coffin.

On April 25, as one stood close to the open grave in the convent of the Franciscan Sisters of São Leopoldo, one could see the serious and sad faces of the religious and students. The white coffin was lowered gently into the grave. The students wept and threw flowers upon it. These were their youthful demonstrations of veneration and gratitude.

"A precious seed confided to the earth for a glorious resurrection." This was how the chaplain of St. Joseph's College, Father Leonardo Müller, S. J., referred to the mortal remains of the saintly nun as the earth began to fall upon the coffin. When the grave was filled, the priestly hand made above the fresh earth the Sign of the Cross, the symbol of our Divine Redeemer's victory. By her love for Our Lord on the Cross, Cecy had triumphed over sin. By this love for Jesus Crucified she was led to the generous fulfillment of her mission as a victim soul.

If you have enjoyed this book, consider making your next selection from among the following . . .